CISTERCIAN STUDIES SERIES: NUMBER ONE HUNDRED NINETY FIVE

André Louf

GRACE CAN DO MORE
Spiritual Accompaniment & Spiritual Growth

CISTERCIAN STUDIES SERIES: NUMBER ONE HUNDRED NINETY FIVE

GRACE CAN DO MORE

by André Louf ocso

Spiritual Accompaniment

&

Spiritual Growth

Translated by Susan Van Winkle

✛

Cistercian Publications
Kalamazoo, Michigan

Originally published as *La grâce peut davantage*.
Paris: Desclée de Brouwer, 1992.

*The work of Cistercian Publications
is made possible in part by support from Western Michigan University
to The Institute of Cistercian Studies*

Available from

cistercian publications
Editorial Offices and Customer Service
Institute of Cistercian Studies
Western Michigan University
Kalamazoo, MI 49008

British and European Customer Service
97 Loughborough Road
Thringstone, Coalville, Leic. LE67 8LZQ

http://www.spencerabbey.org/cistpub/

Typeset by Gale Akins in *Méridien*
Humble Hills Press,
Kalamazoo, MI

PRINTED IN THE UNITED STATES OF AMERICA

TABLE *of* CONTENTS

AUTHOR'S PREFACE

THE FOLLOWING PAGES are the fruit of many courses held successively in Canada, Belgium, and Ireland for those charged with the formation of monks and nuns. A first draft, made from taped conferences, was circulated in French and in English by the Canadian Religious Conference in manuscript form, under the title Spiritual accompaniment (Ottawa 1986). Excerpts reworked by the author formed a chapter of his book *Inspelen op Genade* (Lannoo, Tielt 1983; French translation: *Au gré de sa grâce,* Desclée de Brouwer, Paris 1989), certain aspects of which inspired the present book.

Except for the first chapter—which attempts to describe the place of spiritual accompaniment within the diverse charisms given by the Lord Jesus to his Church—these pages are meant to be descriptive, to fall somewhere between spiritual reflections and an introductory textbook. They may sometimes even give the impression of providing witness, and for this they are indebted to all those the author has had the grace to meet.

Although generally accepted data from depth psychology are freely used here, the informed reader will notice that the author is not a professional in this field. The connections, comparisons, and interpretations that he may propose are subject to verification. Most of the time they are the fruit of fraternal exchanges with other accompanists or with a few professionals. Extremely precious among these latter are the confidence and friendship of two psychiatrists allied in faith and sharing the same interest in every human being's richness and distress.

The reader will also notice all these pages owe to those first spiritual masters—some of whom are still among us—

who dared to let the experience of faith dialogue with the earliest interpretations of it by human sciences: Louis Beirnaert, André Godin, Raymond Hostie, Françoise Dolto, Denis Vasse, Maurice Bellet, to mention only a few; and last but not least, to Dr Fred Blum, priest of the Church of England and psychotherapist, as well as the entire team around him and with him until his death, who were able to accompany and 'save' so many believers of all denominations in the unforgettable country house located in Sutton Courtenay near Oxford in England.

The author of these lines grew up in the monastic tradition, more specifically in the cistercian tradition. His audiences have been composed mainly of monks and nuns, Christians vowed to the contemplative life. By the nature of things, his own practice was incessantly nourished and enlightened by the great texts from that tradition. It would, however, be inexact to think that these pages present a more typically 'monastic' method or a spirituality which can easily be distinguished from a way of spiritual accompaniment more adapted to an active ministry. On the contrary, in an age when all the specific traditions are rereading their founding texts in the light of a renewed spiritual experience, differences fade and the essential traits of the same experience are easily identified from both directions, beyond oppositions which the course of the ages perhaps artificially accentuated. Only far from the sources do people like to cultivate differences. The more we return to the sources, the more we recognize our similarities to each other in the one Lord and in the same paths of his Spirit.

One more word to justify the title *Grace Can Do More*. It comes from a personal memory which I hope I may be permitted to recount here. It represents a sort of saying, not from the lips of some Desert Father, but from a contemporary cardinal, a great servant of the Church during Vatican II, Cardinal Achille Liénart, bishop of Lille. It was spoken on the day of my abbatial blessing, during the festive meal in the monastic refectory. At the beginning of the meal, I had asked to have a certain text by Fénelon, the cardinal's predecessor at Cambrai, read, a text that had always been dear to my heart. In it, the author warns against certain indiscreet directors' habit of going before grace when they should only follow it. Here is an excerpt:

> A director, if he is full of the Spirit of God, never goes before grace in anything. He only follows it patiently, step by step, after testing it with many precautions . . . The things that God makes us do for love of him are usually prepared by a gentle and imperceptible providence which leads things so naturally that they seem to come as if of themselves. There must be nothing forced or irregular . . . We should ask only in the measure in which God gives.

When the reading of the text was finished, the Cardinal turned towards the very young abbot that I was and—in the particularly affectionate tone which was his and which I shall never forget, like a father bequeathing to his son a share of his wisdom—said to me: 'Dear Father Abbot, that is indeed what you will have to do from now on. Never try to impose yourself on your brothers. Of course, you would do very well, but grace can do more!'

There no doubt is the secret of all spiritual accompaniment : never impose yourself on another person, even if you would do 'very well', because 'grace can do more'.

ABBREVIATIONS USED IN THE NOTES

CF   The Cistercian Fathers Series. Spencer, Massachu-
setts, Kalamazoo, Michigan.

CS   The Cistercian Studies Series. Spencer, Kalamazoo.

PL   J.P. Migne, Patrologia cursus completus
series Latina

RB   Regula Benedicti, Saint Benedict's Rule for
Monasteries

SC   Bernard of Clairvaux, *Sermones in Cantica*
(Sermons on the Song of Songs).
Critical edition: Jean Leclercq, H. M. Rochais,
C. H. Talbot, *Sancti Bernardi Opera,*
volumes 1 and 2. Rome: Editiones Cistercienses,
1957, 1958. Translated by Kilian Walsh ocso
and Irene Edmonds, *Bernard of Clairvaux:*
On the Song of Songs, 4 volumes. Kalamazoo:
Cistercian Publications, 1971, 1976, 1979, 1980.

André Louf

GRACE CAN DO MORE
Spiritual Accompaniment & Spiritual Growth

Spiritual Accompaniment in Christian Experience Today 1

THE FIRST PURPOSE of this book is practical: to describe as closely as possible what is now called the relationship or 'dialogue' of spiritual accompaniment. We will reflect on all that constitutes it—humanly, psychologically, and spiritually. What is the goal of spiritual accompaniment? How is someone initiated? In what sense can we use the vocabulary of fatherhood? How can we facilitate dialogue and harmoniously join listening and speaking? What is the nature of the relationship formed between the person accompanied and the one accompanying? In what does the traditional 'opening of the heart', also called 'manifestation of thoughts' consist? What false noises can be heard, what interference comes into play and gets in the way, sometimes without the two partners' knowledge, sometimes a more or less transparent and subtle connivance between them? Any dialogue inevitably includes certain traps which it is useful to be able to manage, not always in order to avoid them, but to know how to recognize them and learn to live with them.

Before any other consideration, however, the very nature of spiritual accompaniment requires a preliminary explanation of its place in, and a determination of its importance to, christian experience. Indeed, the question of spiritual accompaniment lets us discover a crossroads at which several essential elements of the life of faith converge, meet, and intersect. This complexity is enlightened by a global vision of the christian experience: the experience of the individual believer and that of the whole Church.

BETWEEN FLESH AND SPIRIT

To become convinced of the importance of discernment and spiritual accompaniment in all spiritual experience, we need only reread a few well-known verses of chapter eight in Saint Paul's Letter to the Romans which resound like the charter of christian life–of any christian life that is, taken in the widest sense, quite apart from any specific vocation: 'As for you, you are not in the flesh', says Saint Paul, 'but in the Spirit, because the Spirit of God dwells in you.' A little further on, he is more specific:

> Thus, my brothers, we are debtors, not to the flesh to live according to the flesh, because if you live according to the flesh you will die, but if by the Spirit you put to death the works of the flesh, you will live. Indeed, all those who are moved by the Spirit of God are sons of God. You have not received a spirit of slaves to return into fear. You have received a Spirit of adopted sons which makes us cry: Abba, Father! . . . In the same way the Spirit comes to help our weakness, because we do not know how to pray as we ought; but the Spirit himself intercedes for us with unutterable groanings' *(Rm 8:12-15, 26)*.

Here in the first years of Christianity there is an already very precise and detailed description of the christian experience, from the pen of one of the greatest disciples. Paul is perfectly conscious that he is constantly being forced to choose between what he calls 'living according to the flesh' and 'living according to the Spirit'. In the first instance, he would let himself 'be led by the flesh', and in the second, he is 'led by the Spirit'. But how can he choose, since both alternatives seem partially to elude his consciousness? Paul explicitly says that we do not know how to pray, but it is the Spirit who prays in us by groanings which are ineffable or unutterable. This is because the urging, or desire, of the Spirit is at work in us, even when we do not notice, even when his groanings in us are heard and interpreted only by God, because only God searches the heart *(Rom 8:26-27)*.

In these few lines, the Apostle gives us a fairly precise description of christian experience with its unavoidable share of mystery because it places us in contact with God's own life and with its share of the ambiguity which is always possible. He will make this ambiguity explicit in Chapter 5 of the Letter to the Galatians: 'Listen to me: walk according to the Spirit and you will no longer accomplish the desires of the flesh. Because the flesh and its desires is opposed to the Spirit and the Spirit to the flesh; these are opposed to each other so that you may not do what you want' *(Gal 5:16-17)*. How better to express the pangs and the dismay which the Spirit-flesh tension causes in every Christian than not to know how to pray as we ought or do what we want? This vocabulary was not invented by Paul. It comes from the mouth of Jesus, who first used it at one of the most decisive moments of his journey towards Easter to describe what he himself was experiencing in this sinful humanity which he put on to save us: 'Watch and pray so as not to fall into the power of temptation. The spirit is willing, but the flesh is weak' *(Mt 26:41)*.

The Christian's present situation is thus illuminated: it implies tensions and struggles. From his baptism on, the believer is in all truth given over to the Holy Spirit and under his influence. In us, the Spirit works tirelessly, most of the time without the baptized person's knowledge, because we are apparently incapable of becoming conscious of it. But another force and activity still remain in us, one not easy to localize or identify and one whichs mark our whole existence with insurmountable ambiguity. It is this dynamism, different from the life of the Spirit, which Paul calls 'flesh'.

This must not lead us into error. In Saint Paul's writings and in all the New Testament, opposing the spirit to the flesh does not mean opposing the spirit or soul of man to the human body. On the contrary, spirit and flesh are two spiritual notions which can affect body or soul indistinguishably. A body can be fleshly or spiritual. So can the soul. Our whole christian existence takes place both in the flesh and in the Spirit, which makes the discernment between the two especially difficult. We are destined to let ourselves be led by the Spirit, but we can also be at the mercy of the flesh. Moved by the spirit, or at the mercy of the flesh, how can we distinguish between the two, concretely? Obviously, this is one of the most fundamental challenges of christian life and no doubt one of the most urgent in concrete life. Any christian life, both from the point of view of the individual and that of the community, depends on the more or less correct way of living out this antagonism and discerning the true master of the game. Either someone is truly at the 'mercy' of the Spirit: letting himself be led by him *(Rom 8:14)* and taught by his gentle anointing, as Saint John so wonderfully puts it in his First Letter *(1 Jn 2:27)*, and then everything is possible, even the impossible, the improbable or the miraculous! Or, on the contrary, he is at the mercy of the flesh: and then the door is opened to all kinds of illusion, even while someone believes that he is led by the Spirit! It is no wonder that preoccupation with the right choice appears on the very first pages of the New Testament, particularly in Saint Paul and Saint John. Indeed, this problem is a great one and raises the crucial question of knowing whether or not it is possible to verify for ourselves an experience of faith in fidelity to the Holy Spirit's guidance.

Already clearly posed in the New Testament, this problem never ceased being posed over and over again in a particularly fruitful literary history, and by the constancy of comments about spiritual discernment being progressively distilled into a traditional teaching. Although the terminology has evolved over the centuries and emphases have certainly shifted, it is nevertheless true that the body of doctrine, progressively enriched by the experience of many spiritual persons, has remained stable and constant. One might even say that this tradition is, in a certain sense, consubstantial and connatural to the Church, and that it is one of its most precious treasures. The relationship between spiritual experience and the psychological structure of the soul as it was represented during various eras on the one hand, the relationship between the effort of the natural faculties and the intervention of grace on the other hand, finally the recognition by certain proven signs of the equilibrium of all these elements interacting—all has been subjected to reflection and benefited from the experience of the mystics and their shepherds. This is not the place to retrace its history, even in brief. We need only emphasize briefly its marvelous richness.

PUT ON THE BACK BURNER AND BROUGHT TO THE FOREFRONT AGAIN

Yet we must ask the following question: are we worthy heirs of so prestigious a tradition? The answer must be very nuanced. We are permitted to think that, speaking generally, the period in the history of spirituality which is about to end has not particularly shone in that respect. Not that the tradition of spiritual discernment has entirely disappeared from the Church. Far from it. Without speaking of the Society of Jesus, which in this area has remained faithful to the Ignatian method, it is certain that spiritual accompaniment–more often called spiritual direction–has been effectively practiced by a number of priests and religious, and with spiritual fruits which no one could deny. Monasteries of contemplatives no doubt deserve to be particularly mentioned in this respect, because an authentic contemplative experience is difficult to imagine without a minimum of initiation and quality accompaniment. In sum, however, and after important personal or communitarian choices options have been exercised, the life of the Church does not seem to have been affected significantly by the exigencies of rigorous spiritual discernment. There is only one question which would really have been worthwhile: is the subject who is about to choose truly led by the Spirit, was not always explicitly posed, and sometimes even subtly avoided. And this without any ill will. The conclusions of an apparently rigorous rational analysis, combined with an excess of generosity which sometimes masked unarticulated psychological deficiencies, sometimes took the place of the impulse of the Holy Spirit.

This is not the place to analyze why discernment was put on the back burner. We need only recall briefly one of the causes, because it is still very present in the memory of Christians formed before Vatican II and their pastors. It is part of those imponderables which have disappeared somewhat abruptly since the Council, but whose effects are still felt in a widespread and more or less unconscious Catholic culture in Western countries. Moreover, it is less a cause than a symptom, the analysis and diagnosis of which would require deeper research.

To give it a name, let us call it the excessive rationalization of morality. We have already understood that morality and spiritual discernment are not very far from each other, that they often seem to touch and sometimes impinge one on the other, without ever completely covering the same ground. Seen from another point of view, these two areas are clearly detached, strictly opposed to each other; the domain of morality unfolds principally in the world of concepts and principles, and spiritual discernment almost exclusively in the field. The first is inspired by a doctrinal coherence of a sort; the second listens entirely to the action of grace. In spite of this, they cannot help meeting and intersecting. The risk of telescoping, whether by collusion or pure and simple substitution, one with the other remains real.

What are we to understand by this excessive rationalization of morality? Let us concede that there is room for an essentially rational morality, whether it be philosophical or theological, and that this rationalization is indispensable if we want to be able to share this morality with others and transmit rules or principles of behavior to them. Christian morality is no different. In its turn, it can be reduced to a set of principles, some of which repeat verbatim the injunctions of the Old or New Testament and which the moralist can truly consider unchangeable. These principles keep their value. No matter what the decision of a believer struggling with a moral dilemma, his behavior will always be reducible to these principles, at least to a certain point. But for all that, can we maintain that his discernment must purely and simply be limited to a more or less correct application of this moral code? Surely not. Let us not simplify things. In fact, the real question to ask at the time of discernment, the only one which is worth the trouble, is of a different order. It is not as important to know if the decision will conform to a rule laid down by moralists, but rather to have the concrete experience of the Spirit's leading at the core of some decision. From that moment, the real question is of this order: what is the real nature of the desire by which I am being led— insofar as such a discernment is possible—and to what extent can this desire be concretely assumed by the impulse of the Holy Spirit within my soul.

During a certain period, which we may consider as covering the greater part of the nineteenth century and the beginning of the twentieth, moral choice became reduced to the application of certain rules of morality as they had been organized in Moral Theology. Conduct seems to have yielded to legalism: one attempts to conform to a body of rules as one conforms to a law in secular life. And just as whenever the application of the laws becomes thorny a hierarchy of laws is established and jurisprudence created, an analogous phenomenon happened in christian morality. Whatever the principles' obviousness or accuracy, their application became ever more complicated—whether the cases became increasingly singular and unique or the application of these moral laws ran into contradictions which at first glance seem insurmountable. Never mind! Here again, a jurisprudence tended to crop up, leaning, not on this or that court of justice, but on the authority of one textbook author or another. It was to resolve such concrete, seemingly inextricable, situations and to promote a certain practical jurisprudence that the subtle game of the 'moral dilemma' was invented—dilemmas which were both the torment and the entertainment of young clerics, several decades ago thankfully. And just as an able lawyer can manage by great arguments to defend before a civil court just about any interpretation of the law, the moralist in turn can justify almost any doubtful behavior. This is the fate of, among others, dictatorship, war, terrorism, torture, and even abortion or other proven crimes. The most convincing argument was no doubt that of the debate for or against contraception, in which pastors and theologians confronted one another with almost equally valid arguments until the Holy See took a clearer position. Maybe this is the proof by contradiction that such a rationalization of morality ends in a deadlock, even on the level of principles.

The justification of these various points of view was facilitated all the more in that such debates of principles, and in particular the famous moral dilemmas which were supposed to illustrate them, were completely abstract and did not relate at all to the concrete persons who could have been their real subjects. In the dilemmas' scenarios, these persons were given purely fictitious and thus perfectly interchangeable names: Titius and Titia, Caius and Caia, when it was a question of sexual morality—a subject which recurred often. The moral dilemma had become a purely abstract case devoid of any consistency, sometimes of any plausibility, and was applied nowhere except in the realm of ideas and principles. We were far from giving inner attention to the desire of the Holy Spirit, patiently and progressively adapting to the concrete possibilities of each individual. Discernment was content with a clear vision of the principles under debate, and came to a verdict based on competent authorities, which only needed the good will and generosity of those concerned to be executed with greater or lesser success.

A discernment which did not take into account the complexity of the desires at work in each of us seems to us today suspicious, and rightly so. A change has already begun, partly facilitated by discoveries in the human sciences, especially those of depth psychology. To this subject later we will return. Freud's intuitions, which are now more or less absorbed as part of our general culture, have made us particularly sensitive to the complexity of the desires and tendencies which animate our interior world, to the irritating point of casting suspicion on our apparently most spiritual behavior. Even so, we may think that, when better and better integrated, their contribution will be beneficial for a greater understanding of the spiritual experience. It has already become an element which we can no longer do without.

From this confrontation between the human sciences and the traditional views of spiritual life a greater interest in spiritual accompaniment has sprung up. This interest is shared with others, but has arisen in a different way. Various spiritual movements with the generic name 're-newal' which have begun to spread in the Church also alert us to the urgency of a more rigorous spiritual discernment. When the individual or the group manifests a 'charismatic' behavior, how can we distinguish an innocent overflow of feelings from psychotic swings which risk destructuring the personality? How can we feel the difference between healthy euphoria—a symptom of interior peace—and hysteria or delusions of grandeur? And how can we determine what is the authentic fruit of the

Spirit in the heart of these emotional manifestations en-
coded by each psychology which is engaged and more or
less tried by the impact of the Spirit's intervention? Pastors ask such questions more and more frequently, with
the utter seriousness and gravity that they require.

Forgotten and neglected for a time, spiritual discernment from now on will find its full credit, and it is not an
understatement to say that it seems particularly adapted
to the needs of the Church and to this new outpouring of
the Holy Spirit which good Pope John prayed for following Vatican II. In all the areas of the Church the same
need is felt, whether in the formation of the laity, of future priests, or in monastic and religious life. Everywhere
we are conscious of having gone from the realm of law
and observances to the realm of values and interiority—a
terminology which needs to be made more careful and
precise and a movement which can be truly fruitful only
in the measure that the discernment of the Spirit's movements within the heart of each brother and sister is again
one of the key elements of spiritual experience. The quality of spiritual experience can only gain from this. If it is
correctly exercised, the art of spiritual discernment is infinitely more demanding than any law or observance. In
fact, its aim is to liberate and listen to the Holy Spirit's
interior call within each person, which is never bound or
exhausted by any law or rule. Because if it is really true
that 'grace can do more', we will have an always greater
need for believers who are experts in detecting the subtler
movements of grace, those whom the Letter to the Hebrews calls 'adults in the faith, those whose faculties are
trained by practice to discern good and evil' *(Hb 5:14)*.

DISCERNMENT AND THE WORD OF GOD

We said earlier that spiritual discernment was exercised at the junction of several experiences which are essential for any believer. Let us first state more clearly the link between spiritual discernment and listening to the Word of God. Understanding this link is necessary because this listening is a real key, perhaps even the essential key to all spiritual discernment.

In the oldest monastic literature, we have from the pen of the renowned Evagrius Ponticus (346-399) a little treatise on the combat between the passions, with the greek title *Antirhetikos*, that is the 'Fighter'. In fact, in it Evagrius takes a count of the 'fighting' words by which the monk must fight temptations. These are always verses from the Word of God, which is charged with a spiritual force and energy able to contradict and fight wild desires. Evagrius even went to the trouble of making a double catalogue: on the one hand the desires in question, and on the other an impressive list of scriptural quotations, selected to be at the disposal of monks in their struggle against evil thoughts. Facing each passion, Evagrius built up an arsenal of words from the Bible, words charged with a secret force able to recognize sin where it was hiding and fight it effectively. Such a technique might seem strange to us today, and even a bit simplistic. The fact itself is, however, very suggestive and hides a profound truth which has nothing illusory about it: the Word of God itself is the first tool of good spiritual discernment. It is a key to understanding what is going on in the heart of man. Let us examine this more deeply for a moment.

That the Word of God is a key that opens spiritual discernment means first of all that simply hearing or reading the Word is already an exercise in discernment. To understand the word of the Bible as the Word of God addressed to each one of us today requires discernment because there are many possible interpretations of the Word of God. At first, it necessarily appears to be a human word, very concretely situated in a particular history, language, and literary genre. As a human word, witnessing to a human experience and history, it is relatively easy to understand. Any professional exegete has the tools needed for this. Such a reading however, is not enough. If we deal only with the literary envelope of the biblical Word, its 'letter', as the Fathers used to call it, we have not yet heard anything of what God is telling us now through it. To welcome the Word of God as what it truly is for us, a Word that God addresses to us today, requires a discernment which is the particular secret of what western monks called *lectio divina,* that is, reading the Bible understood as listening to God speak to us through the Bible. Such a discernment presupposes a continuous availability to the Event of the Word of God, an Event which is renewed constantly in the heart of the believing reader, but which remains unknown to anyone who stops at a simple historical exegesis.

A concrete example may enlighten us. When we read in the Old Testament the history of the jewish people, we may find it very commonplace and comparable on almost every point to the vagaries of all the eastern peoples' past destiny. Through this history, another can be discerned, a sacred history led by God: the history of Jesus, come to renew the Covenant in his blood; a history which in its very movement already includes the history of the Church after his Ascension and the history of each believer! Similarly when the believer reads in the Gospel the history of this man called Jesus, who was born in Bethlehem, who lived between Nazareth and Jerusalem, he must discern the presence of God and his action among his people, and not only at the time of Jesus, but also for the new time opened by the Risen Christ. Contrary to what might appear, such readings are not the fruit of an optical illusion or an overly fertile imagination. The uninterrupted presence of the Spirit in the letter of Scripture arouses them

The Event of the Word of God

in us, and the biblical word constantly inspired by the Spirit becomes the Word which God addresses concretely to us today. In this sense, all lectio divina, all true reading of Scripture, implies a continuous exercise of discernment.

Yet this exercise of reading, which is at the disposal of every believing theologian, is not exhausted by the elaboration of a theological meaning of the biblical text for which intelligence enlightened by faith is sufficient. At the heart of *lectio divina* something more important is revealed, a sort of second level of reading which can take place at a deeper level of being and be strictly personal in nature. The Word of God is addressed first to me, a believer of today. This is why discerning the Word of God by the intervention of a human word is given through this Event of the Word which comes addressed to me personally. There is a certain impropriety about calling this meaning which the believer takes from his *lectio divina* 'secondary'. In the order of the believer's experience, this reading is in a certain sense absolutely first, before all the others and the condition for the others. The Event does not leave a person unchanged: the Word of God listened to reaches the heart, makes it move and leap, producing the special fruit of a greater sensitivity to the movement of the Holy Spirit.

In general, this new sensitivity is given, not in advance, but only at the very heart of this reading of the Word. It is the Word, in fact, which gives the capacity to discern it. In the greek patristic tradition, it was said that the Word makes its reader *dioratikos,* literally : 'one who knows how to look through things, who is able to discern'. The author of the Letter to the Hebrews has left us an impressive and colorful description of this extraordinary power of the Word:

> Indeed, the word of God is living and effective, sharper than a two-edged sword, penetrating even between soul and spirit, joints and marrow, and able to discern

> reflections and thoughts of the heart. No
> creature is concealed from him, but every-
> thing is naked and exposed to the eyes of
> him to whom we must render an account.
> *(Hb 4:12-13)*

This text is crucial. It is truly the sovereign Word of God
itself which touches the heart, wounds it, and by wounding it wakes it, making it sensitive and perceptive. In
christian life in general, and especially in a life ordered to
contemplation, daily habitual reading of the Word of God
in the form of *lectio divina* is the place *par excellence* for discernment. By listening with his heart to the Word of God
for a long time, any believer can learn to listen to his own
heart, to perceive an echo of the Word which echoes and
is reflected within him. At the same time, his heart is
awakened by the Word. It dilates, grows to the full dimension of the Word and Sacred History. Encountered in the
intimacy of his heart, the believing subject becomes a
'hearer' a 'seer', and begins or continues his apprenticeship in discernment. This interior growth gives a person
indwelt by the Word a 'prophetic' heart in the strongest
sense of the word. This is a heart able to interpret any
historical event in the light of Sacred History. Habitual reading of the Word gives him a new sensitivity. Irradiated by
the power which emanates from the Word of God, this
reading continuously refines a spiritual sense which progressively enables the believer to perceive the Event of salvation hidden behind every historical event, humankind's
and his own.

   In the work of receptive listening to the movements of
the Holy Spirit in the life of the brothers and sisters who
come to him, the person who accompanies is guided in
this task by an interior sensitivity attuned to the Holy Spirit.
This is not fundamentally different from the spiritual sensitivity with which he has already learned to listen and
savor the Word of God. Let us even dare to say that these

two sensitivities—the two interior 'anointings', to use the vocabulary of the *First Letter of Saint John (2:27)*—are one and coincide perfectly. The heart which leaps when touched by a Word of God in Scripture is the same heart which is moved and similarly leaps when, through the words and feelings shared by a brother or sister, something of the desire of the Holy Spirit who is at work in them is manifested to the one accompanying them.

SPIRITUAL DISCERNMENT AND CONVERSION

While making this quick inventory of the spiritual realities which affect spiritual discernment, we must spend a few moments on the grace of conversion. The New Testament refers to this by the greek word *metanoïa*, literally: 'turning of the *noûs'*—a word translated here as 'spirit' or 'heart'. In truth, the work of spiritual discernment cannot be conceived unless a person allows himself to be led by an untiring movement of conversion. Let us recall a famous text from Saint Paul: 'Do not conform yourself to this age but be transformed by the renewal of your mind, that you may discern what is the will of God, what is good and pleasing and perfect' *(Rm 12:2)*. This is one of the most explicit New Testament texts to praise discernment, underline its absolute necessity, and at the same time put it in close relation to conversion.

This is not the only passage in which Paul mentions both spiritual discernment and the necessity of our knowing clearly the will of God. It is often the object of his prayer on behalf of his recipients: that they may know the perfect will of God for them *(Rm 12:2; Eph 5:17; Col 1:9)*. In the text just quoted, Paul reminds us that such discernment depends upon an *anakaïnôsis tou noôs,* a renewal of the *noûs.* We may understand this term to mean the seat of spiritual intuition in man. It is borrowed from greek philosophical vocabulary, and no translation into modern languages is completely satisfactory. Some translate it 'intellect', but this word, with its intellectual overtones, is misplaced in the context, because this tone is completely foreign to Paul's thought and that of the New Testament. One might translate it appropriately 'spirit' or even better perhaps 'heart'. Indeed, this 'renewal of the *noûs'* recommended by Paul implies the awakening of the heart of which we spoke in the previous paragraph. The Apostle is trying to say that the ability to discern the will of God requires a new spiritual sensitivity, precisely the one which is given to us through the event of our conversion. Besides, this conversion does not concern only the heart. Its reach is anthropological, in the strongest meaning of the word; it concerns the whole of man. At the heart of his conversion, he has become another. He has 'put on the new man' to echo Saint Paul's terminology *(Eph 4:24),* that is, he has received a new status by being recreated in the Holy Spirit. The Spirit's action will never end, and the first conversion is still only a beginning whose consequences are unpredictable. The new human condition thus received is destined to grow and evolve endlessly. It is the same for spiritual discernment, which is also called to grow constantly and become progressively more refined. Thus there is the continual sense of always going forward, from beginning to beginning, God unceasingly giving and untiringly increasing his gift.

Such a gift is perhaps far more widespread than we might think. Its nature is such that it is possible to share it among brothers and sisters and to receive in return the gifts each one of them has received. Indeed, it may happen that, during an exchange, the partners reach a depth of sharing which suddenly makes them aware that the experience of the discernment received by both, and from which the whole dynamic of the exchange had begun, was similar. In a less dazzling but no less real way, this spiritual sensitivity unique to each person comes to life in varying degrees in Christians who care about deepening the experience of their faith. In this way, we may think that each brother or sister has already received some first fruits of this gift in the form of a kind of interior sensitivity of which they are not always aware and of which they may be wary, sometimes without reason. Such sensitivity allows them to glimpse what others do not yet suspect, and will not until it pleases God to open the eyes of their heart, but what at the time is appropriate for them. Indeed, God ardently desires to awaken all believers to this grace of discernment, to give them the same ability to be in tune with the gift of the Spirit in their heart. Now there is a secret connivance between those who already see a little bit. They recognize each other by a certain transparency of language and feelings, by the same wavelength on which they express themselves. This last point is not negligible, because the starting point from which a person speaks and shares will be different for someone who is starting to see and someone who does not yet see. With experience, it can become relatively simple during a conversation to realize from which interior place—or on which wavelength, if you like—the speaker is expressing himself. One can take as a starting point one's knowledge, intelligence, natural intuition and finesse, generosity—all excellent things which can sometimes dispose us for the gift of discernment. One can also express oneself from the heart in a state of watchfulness whose deep life overflows and radiates unceasingly.

As we will see a bit later, it is not the words or rational messages which are important in spiritual dialogue, but the life which overflows from the heart: 'The mouth speaks from the fullness of the heart', Jesus reminds us *(Mt 12:34)*. During an exchange, it is possible to be convinced and convincing, and even to reveal oneself as forceful on the level of language, without transmitting life to one's partner. And on the other hand, a single very sober and simple word, apparently unremarkable and insignificant, without any oratorical brilliance, yet pronounced from a heart

truly renewed in the Holy Spirit, is able to turn someone around decisively and bring to birth in him the life
of God. The condition is simple: interior renewal must
be constant in the speaker. In this sense, spiritual accompaniment is continual conversion, not only of the
one accompanied, but first and foremost of the one who
accompanies.

Spiritual discernment and obedience

There is an obvious link between obedience and spiritual discernment. It supposes that someone is ready to
renounce one's own desires to welcome the desire of
God. One must be able to perceive the will of God correctly. Experience has taught us that recognizing this
desire is not immediately obvious. The last chapter of
this book will deal with this in more depth, but it is
useful to mention it here.

It was generally accepted that in matters of accompaniment—or spiritual direction, as we used to call it—the
obedience of the one directed was far more important than
other dispositions and guaranteed the complete success
of the operation. It was enough to obey, they used to say,
and all would be for the best. This statement is far from
being false. It contains a deep truth, but on the condition
that it not be interpreted in too simplistic a manner. Only
a true discernment can permit a fully christian obedience,
that is to say, one which reproduces the obedience of Christ,
which agrees to go where Christ himself went in the mystery of his Passion: 'He was obedient to death' *(Ph 2:8).*
This can come only from an obedience which engages a
certain depth of being. Not all forms of obedience reach
that depth. For example, the respect due the traffic code
is an act of elementary prudence and common sense; it
implies a civic correctness, an obedience. Yet we cannot
call this a prolongation of the celebration of the Passion of

Christ! It is in this sense that many kinds of obedience formed behaviors without implying spiritual reasons for them. On the other hand, consenting to obey in the name of the Gospel cannot be done outside the Passion of Christ or without this obedience becoming a real participation in his death and resurrection. By obeying in this way, the Passion of Christ is celebrated. In the strongest sense of the word, the believer is affected by this obedience in the deepest layers of his being, and it is impossible for him not to be deeply transformed by it.

The metamorphosis which can take place in obedience implies, however, that this not be a caricature, but authentically spiritual, in the sense that the work of discernment belongs as much to the one commanding to the one obeying. Both are constantly subject to discernment. This involvement of them both is very demanding. It is still true that obedience is not only the basis of all religious life but of all christian life. It is no less true that it has sometimes been grossly simplified, reduced to a useful little tactic which gave the one obeying the assurance that he would never make a mistake and would always have 'peace of conscience'. Even if the saying 'One who obeys is sure that he will never make a mistake' is perfectly valid, it is only at the very deep level of inner experience that discernment is established. It can never sanction a lack of true commitment in this sense. This would produce only a caricature of obedience, at best the obedience of the Pharisee of the Gospel, the 'just man' trying to justify himself by the almost military rigor of his submission.

Evangelical obedience, on the other hand, forces us to take a new look at ourselves and commits our freedom. It participates in a real drama—and God knows that this can hurt sometimes!—but it is a saving drama: it is Redemption in action. Far from being content to allow us to be 'correct', evangelical obedience permits us to be saved through many heartbreaks and alternations between darkness and light. In a word: it permits us to be deeply trans-

formed and to become new creatures, endowed with a
new sensitivity and a new way of looking at things. In the
heart of obedience, as crucifying and sometimes 'blind' as
it may be, arises a new way of looking which lets us see
clearly. No doubt this is the grain of truth contained in the
advice which often used to be given to anyone who had
some difficulty aligning himself with the will of a superior: 'Start by obeying, you will understand later.' Even if
such a sentence might have been abused in practice, it
expresses much more than a simple common sense fact.
It is verified first at the level of spiritual discernment, which
we are speaking of here. It means: 'Obey first, because
renouncing your own will manifests the will of God to
you'. It is obedience that gives discernment and makes
everything luminous.

SPIRITUAL DISCERNMENT AND PRAYER

Spiritual discernment joins two other important aspects
of christian experience: prayer and action. Prayer holds
first place: both the place where discernment is the most
necessary and the place where we may easily learn it. Saint
Paul tells us that we are not even able to say 'Jesus is the
Christ' unless we are helped by the Holy Spirit *(1 Cor 12:3)*.
Similarly, when someone starts to pray, the Spirit is not
only at work in him, but the Spirit precedes him in prayer.
Saint Paul also says explicitly: 'We do not know how to
pray as we ought, but it is he, the Spirit himself who in-
tercedes for us with inexpressible groanings' *(Rm 8:26)*.
Prayer is a kind of discernment in action, to the degree
that it consists essentially in abandoning oneself progressively to the Spirit's prayer in us each time that it comes
up, a little at a time, to the surface of our consciousness.
    This is one of the most thrilling but also one of the most
puzzling mysteries of christian experience. On the one
hand, we could say that we literally bathe in the light of

the Holy Spirit and in his prayer at work within us. On the other hand, we must admit that the echoes of it which we perceive are extremely rare. It remains true, nevertheless, that God has destined us to perceive some echo. It is he who will patiently teach us to seize and interpret the interior movement of the Spirit in our heart. Like *lectio divina*, private prayer becomes a very appropriate place for spiritual discernment; it is both the source and the norm of discernment. The interior sensitivity which will allow us to have a slight premonition about what God is doing in someone else is exactly the same sensitivity which lets us perceive the Holy Spirit urging us to pray and putting into our hearts the very words of our prayer; and the same sensitivity which gives us a deep sense of the Word of God.

John of the Cross, as the experienced guide in the ways of prayer he was, often insisted on the necessity of discernment in someone who is called to guide others in the ways of prayer. What might be of some help to such a guide is not what he thinks he knows because he learned it in books. God's intervention is never programmed in advance, and the guide must be able to feel God at work, even when he seems to leave the well-worn path and ask the unexpected. John of the Cross even seems harsh towards those accompanists who have at their disposal no other means besides some easy recipes that have been successful in other circumstances, or general principles of spiritual theology, or even simple common sense. All this is not enough: the great misfortune for contemplatives, he writes in his Commentary on the third stanza of *The Living Flame of Love*, is letting themselves be guided by another blind man.

> It is of great importance for the soul that desires to profit, and not to fall back, to consider in whose hands it is placing itself; for as is the master, so will be the disciple, and as is the father, so will be the son. There

is hardly anyone who in all respects will
guide the soul perfectly along the highest
stretch of the road, or even along the in-
termediate stretches, for it is needful that
such a guide should be wise and discreet
and experienced . . .If a guide have no experience of the higher part of the road, he
will be unable to direct the soul therein,
when God leads it so far. A guide might
even do the soul great harm if, not himself
understanding the way of the spirit, he
should cause the soul, as often happens, to
lose the unction of these delicate ointments,
wherewith the Holy Spirit gradually pre-
pares it for Himself, and if instead of this
he should guide the soul by other and lower
paths of which he has read here and there,
and which are suitable only for beginners.
Such guides know no more than how to
deal with beginners–please God they may
know even so much!–and refuse to allow
souls to go beyond these rudimentary acts
of meditation and imagination, even
though God is seeking to lead them far-
ther, so that they may never exceed or de-
part from their natural capacity, whereby
they can achieve very little.[2]

Saint John of the Cross shows himself here perfectly conscious of the distance between what he calls the 'natural
activity' of the soul, for which a common sense counsel
can be enough, and the interior urging of the Holy Spirit
which, at a given moment of the inner experience, takes
over from natural activity. Being experienced in the ways
of the Spirit does not imply, however, that the guide runs on

2. *Sermo 17.2 on the Song of Songs.*

ahead on the spiritual way along which the person accompanied is traveling. Each way is unique and cannot be anticipated or repeated. The accompanist must, however, have received the inner sensitivity to let him recognize the action of God in another person. Now, the signs of God's action or his traces in prayer are generally very faint. John of the Cross spoke of 'delicate perfumes', scarcely perceptible but secretly present in a heart in which the grace of the Spirit is at work. It very often happens that God is urging the one accompanied in a direction different from the accompanist's direction. It doesn't matter. He is not even called to follow his brothers on the road where grace is waiting for them but not him. He is simply asked to be able to recognize their path and the direction along which God is gently guiding them. Besides, it can happen that God is as apparently disconcerting to the accompanist as to the one accompanied, or that God seems to draw them into a darkness where all the landmarks of knowledge disappear and where both feel utterly distraught. Whether this occurs in prayer or in action, the only thing important then is to recognize the hand of God, even if we have the impression that all is lost and that we are about to lose ourselves. The impression, and even the quasi-certitude, that we are no longer advancing, that we are desperately stagnating, is not at all important. It is enough to be able to discern the meaning that God intends to give to what is apparently a failure and to the sense of frustration which springs from it. All apparent death is a promise of new life, and to recognize the glimmers of this new life through temporary death is precisely the chief job of spiritual discernment.

SPIRITUAL DISCERNMENT IN ACTION

At first sight the other pole of christian life, action, seems opposed to prayer. This is only a superficial view. Action is no less important than prayer, even in a life style which is exclusively contemplative, because the solitary often finds himself very much engaged in all kinds of activities which are indispensable to his subsistence, and also by the very nature of spiritual discernment, which constitutes a common ground between prayer and action. In fact, what is really important, in prayer as in action, is to be truly under the influence of the Spirit. This sensitivity to the Spirit can be learned in prayer as well as in action. What has been learned during prayer time will facilitate the discovery of God's action at the time of action; similarly, what is learned about the activity of God in the heart of action will facilitate listening to the Spirit at the time of prayer. In both cases, what is important is to be in a state of waiting and to take an attitude of listening, examining, scanning the signs of the Holy Spirit.

At this depth, paradoxically, their very distinction—rather than a fundamental interaction between prayer and action—is abolished. Both are held in hand, and let themselves be guided by the same inner sensitivity. At a given moment, spiritual discernment means 'inner attentiveness to the movement of the Spirit who urges us to prayer'; at another moment, it will be 'attention to what the same Spirit urges to do concretely'. We touch here a place where the contemplative and the apostle merge in each believer.

Maybe this is the meaning of the recommendation Saint Ignatius of Loyola gave his companions when he asked them to be *in actione contemplativus,* 'a contemplative in the very heart of action'. Surely, this does not mean confusing action with contemplation, or claiming, as one sometimes hears, that action can substitute for contemplation and even do without it. On the contrary, it means to learn to act peacefully, in such a way that the inner ear remains always listening for the movement of the Holy Spirit and that action lets itself continually be guided by these movements. The examination of conscience that the same Ignatius proposed to his disciples has no other meaning. Whereas after the founder's death, it was assimilated to a sort of accounting of actions accomplished, omitted, or perfectible, in the spirit of Saint Ignatius it was quite otherwise. The particular *examen* is, above all, for him a moment of deep recollection, when all activity is stopped for an instant, in the middle and at the end of the day, or even several times during the day. Its goal is listening to one's heart to perceive the signs of the Spirit's inward urging and to verify if one's outward activity is still attuned to it. We can understand the importance of these inward turnings; they permit the most committed apostle constantly to retune his human activity to the Spirit's urging, as he is capable of hearing it in his heart. Thus, at a very deep human level, the most contemplative prayer and the most dedicated activity, dedicated first of all in the Spirit and welling up from him, are practically identical. Is this not the mystery which so many saints have lived and witnessed to?

The New Testament uses a variety of images to describe this secret activity of the Holy Spirit in the heart of each believer: the Spirit's groanings *(Rm 8:26)*, the urging of the Spirit *(Rm 8:6-7)*, the desire of the Spirit *(Rm 8:27)*, the anointing of the Spirit *(1 Jn 2:27)*. In more modern terms, we might compare this to uninterrupted background music, against which all our life, our prayer, and our action unfolds gently and peacefully. When Saint Bernard of Clairvaux wanted to describe how the believer allows himself continually to be guided by this inner sweetness, he used a well-chosen expression—and no doubt he was the first to do so. William of Saint-Thierry, one of the holy abbot's biographers, did not hesitate to apply it to him: the believer,

he says, can act always and at every moment *unctione
magistra*, having as his inner teacher this anointing of
which Saint John speaks in his first Letter *(1 Jn 2:27)²*.
The contemporaries of Saint Bernard remembered him
as a man exceptionally gifted for the ministry of accompaniment and remarkable for his penetrating spiritual
judgment, to which the acuteness of his interior sensitivity disposed him. His secretary, Geoffrey of Auxerre, no
doubt did not wander far from historic truth when he
wrote in a sermon preached on the anniversary of his
death:

> We can scarcely believe . . . how easy it was
> for him to perceive what tormented some,
> what affected the spirit of others: with what
> love he disposed and foresaw everything,
> so that the work would not weigh on one
> or the excess of repose let this other grow
> dull; how affectionately he weighed, if one
> dare say it, even the sleep of each of his
> brothers. It is by a divine instinct, I believe,
> that he had learned to know the strengths,
> the dispositions and even the stomach of
> each, in fact, through Jesus Christ, the true
> servant of all.³

SPIRITUAL ACCOMPANIMENT, A MINISTRY IN THE CHURCH

We have just seen how spiritual accompaniment and discernment intersect a certain number of fundamental
christian realities. From this observation naturally arises a
question: is spiritual accompaniment not one of the
ministries of whose importance in the life of the

2. *Sermo 17.2 on the Song of Songs.*
3. *Sermo in anniversario obitus sancti Bernardi,* 11; PL 185:580.

Church Vatican II reminded us? [4] At one time in history, this ministry was reserved to priests, but this was not always so, and its nature does not require it. It is a charism which is available to everyone, and a ministry which can be exercised by any Christian. It is a precious gift, necessary to the spiritual health of the People of God.

In fact, the ministry of spiritual accompaniment should be considered a natural complement to baptism. The catechumen needed to have a minister present for baptism to be administered. A newly baptized Christian usually needed another minister, an educator in the faith, so that the grace of baptism could bear its full fruit in him. When the sacrament was received, ritual signs were made: immersion and a word spoken by a brother in the faith. In this way, in the faith of the Church, a gesture and a word together have constituted the sacrament which begets new life in Christ. Yet this is still a seed, a sprout called on to grow and develop. The newly baptized must still learn to let this shoot pervade, little by little, all the dimensions of his being, and each time this is so many renewed births. For the full force of the sacrament to unfold its energies in the believer's life, however, it is fitting that this new life be cultivated with appropriate artfulness, to prevent the seed from withering and dying. This is the role of accompaniment which, in this respect, can be seen as an extension of the sacrament of baptism, because it too has the double sign of gesture and word. The gesture or rite is the human relationship woven between the one accompanying and the one accompanied. As for the word, it comes at the right time, spoken by a minister and received as coming from God. We shall see how delicate such a ministry is,

---

4. *Lumen Gentium,* 12: 'The same Holy Spirit...alloting his gifts "to everyone according as he will" (1 Cor 12:11), He distributes special graces among the faithful of every rank. By these gifts He makes them fit and ready to undertake various tasks or offices advantageous for the renewal and upbuilding of the Church.'

and which human and spiritual conditions can, to a certain extent, guarantee its fruit.

Is it even necessary to remember that this is essentially a lay ministry? Nothing in it requires that it be reserved only to men. It finds its roots in baptismal priesthood, and of itself does not require ministerial priesthood. It pertains to a different order than priesthood. Spiritual accompaniment in its own way prolongs the ministry of ordained priests, which culminates in the eucharistic celebration. By and large, there would not be enough priests anyway, and besides, their presence is not indispensable, because accompaniment is exercised within the innumerable bonds of friendship and fraternity which are constantly being woven between the members of the mystical Body of Jesus.

A better knowledge of the history of religious life would show us, if it were still necessary, the degree to which such a ministry was for centuries very widely exercised by laymen and laywomen. It is astounding that those who are promoting the role of women in the Church today have not noticed the eminent role which numerous women played at the head or in the heart of communities of religious women, particularly contemplative communities. This was often an authentic pastoral ministry and a true spiritual maternity, which in themselves do not necessitate sacramental priesthood. Examples in history are abundant.

We could go back even further still, to see this ministry of accompaniment at its very source, where it is exercised naturally: in the heart of every christian home. The way christian parents acquit themselves in their parental ministry is without any doubt related to spiritual accompaniment, especially when it comes to the transmission of faith. Is it not at the heart of the christian home that such a ministry is first learned? Many of those charged with formation in religious life are brought to this realization, *a contrario*, by frequently noticing gaps in the transmission of the faith to their new recruits who, for various reasons, did not receive this correctly in their family home. These gaps lie both in the transmission of the religious heritage itself and in the psychological structure which should favor such transmission. Formation guides often find themselves faced with entirely blank pages which have never been filled. It is true that, in many cases, they still can be, at least partially, as it is also true that spiritual accompaniment can replace with some success what did not occur at the proper time. This observation only confirms the importance of the parents' role, and how a first important step in spiritual accompaniment should take place within the christian family.

Of course, catechism and the appropriate teaching methods it uses are an absolutely necessary intermediary in the transmission of the faith. But this is only a reflection of the experience of faith, incapable of transmitting the experience itself and remedying previous deficiencies. It is only by being a witness that the catechist or the accompanist will be capable of transmitting this experience and filling in those blank pages as much as possible. But this can be done only to the degree that the witness gives himself over in a transparent way to God's action within him. Then he witnesses to the marvels that have happened in him through God's action and can happen in his brothers as well. Such a transmission, founded on the witness of a lived experience, brings us once again to spiritual discernment and the new sensitivity which the Spirit provides to allow us to perceive correctly what happens to us from God. In this sense, a renewed practice of spiritual accompaniment constitutes an opportunity for the Church today. It poses in new and particularly well-adapted terms the problem of an authentic teaching of the life of faith and of spiritual experience.

The Object of Spiritual Accompaniment 2

IGHLIGHTING various implications of spiritual discernment in various aspects of the life of faith has given us a general overview of the question of spiritual accompaniment. One last point deserves our attention before we examine the details more deeply. What is the object of spiritual accompaniment? In other words: what needs to be 'accompanied' in the person who is experiencing christian faith?

The word 'experience' implies another: 'life'. The grace of christian life is essentially a 'life' and, in its strongest sense, a 'movement', 'tension', 'growth', 'tendency' to self-realization, towards complete maturity. Yet life is not without the threat of death, the non-accomplishment of promise. A life can become sickly, paralyzed, it can suffocate and finally be extinguished. Nothing remains immutable because life does not stand still.

If this is the most immediately perceptible apprehension of life in general, we still need to clarify what is included in 'christian life'. To put it in the simplest possible terms: it is this seed of divine life which we also call grace, received at baptism. Let us insist on this word 'seed', which, relative to the word 'life', means that this life is still in embryo in the human person. All that will be in fullness one day, our future development, is already mysteriously present in the seed, though still invisibly. The beneficiary, even if he receives baptism as an adult, does not necessarily perceive its effects with his senses. If he is sanctified down to the root, the more peripheral layers of his being are not instantly transformed. Far from it. Traditional theology has always recognized the survival in the baptized of what it calls 'the consequences of sin'. By this

33

it meant that this seed of life is called to make its way progressively in the human person, through forces which are contrary to, and at first sight seem to be opposed to, this life. It also recognizes that man is a wounded being, and that the traces of his wounds, never erased in one stroke, are present and active in him for a long time.

The development of the seed of life does not follow a consistent course and it inevitably includes some uncertainty, and sometimes painful reverses. Obstacles will crop up on its path, so subtle for some persons that they will need to be recognized with great care, lest illusion—which is always possible—creep in on these occasions. This is one of those essential and easily apprehended aspects of the original wound which each person bears in that he experiences great difficulty in discerning, among many contradictory motions, the desire that truly wells up from the deepest part of his being, that is, from that source within which we call 'divine life'. The wounded person does not hear, does not feel, does not see what of God there is within himself. As he has needed someone else, a brother, to have the seed of divine life planted in his heart through the sacrament of baptism, so he will usually need another, a new, fraternal relationship, for the seed to develop without too many obstacles.

It is worthwhile insisting a bit on this 'vital' character of the spiritual experience, that is, on the fact that it is first of all a 'life', called to grow, to reach fullness, and bear fruit. This should be self-evident, but it is not impossible that we still suffer a little—and sometimes very much—from somewhat restrictive conceptions about christian life which continue to haunt our religious culture today.

It would be infinitely simpler if the experience of faith were reduced to assent to a block of clear and simple absolute truths about God and man, that is, a body of knowledge. In that case, an intelligently formulated catechism, explained by a good catechist using a proven teaching method would be amply sufficient. The believer would be asked only to learn and memorize a certain number of notions, to be able to draw his own logically consequent conclusions in case new problems present themselves, which is within the realm of possibility in a constantly changing society. Then we would need a good theologian or an experienced catechist, not a pedagogue or someone to accompany our life!

It would be just as simple if christian faith could be reduced to a *praxis* ruled by a code of prescriptions and proscriptions, a code to which we would need only conform carefully. Christian experience would then consist fundamentally in the application of a morality founded on a certain number of sound, correct principles. Once again, we would need, not someone to accompany our life, but a convinced moralist, able to resolve by well-tested principles the moral dilemmas which would then present themselves.

It would not be difficult either if the experience of faith consisted mainly in a solid course of pastoral action, in the service of which each person were invited to enroll with some degree of generosity and effectiveness. A good sociologist of religion or a fairly charismatic leader would be enough.

But in fact, christian experience, this life of God in us, will not remain at the 'experiential' level. It will of necessity distill a body of doctrine in which it will become explicit, one which theologians will refine and councils sanction. Yet it is from this very experience that the body of doctrine springs. The experience remains absolutely primary, in every sense. The formulas of faith presuppose it and are illumined by its light. Cut off from this experience and left to themselves, they can never really transmit that experience.

The principles of this christian experience repeat themselves in each person and, accordingly, certain attitudes or external behaviors are inevitably produced. Their constant

elements can be shaped into what we call a moral doctrine and commented upon. Cut off from the experience
unique to each person and, sometimes, reduced to an abstract study of behavior, this morality would have great
difficulty convincing anyone or promoting a real experience of life. Worse, it would have an unfortunate tendency
to harden into a moralizing and self-sufficient legalism.

Finally, the inner experience of faith, which is essentially contagious and always feels an overwhelming need
to spread, will necessarily overflow in activity which bears
witness to brothers and sisters and the world. To remain
true, this witness needs to stay in constant contact with
the experience itself. It is convincing only to the degree
that it springs from experience, overflowing from it, as it
were, and only when it is given without being directly
intended. Not everyone who wants to be a witness can be;
only the person can who knows by experience what he
preaches.

All this must not lead us to suppose that there is some
pointless complexity inherent in the life of faith. On the
contrary. Life is essentially meant to be propagated, so it
should be extremely simple to transmit it. It is not so much
a matter of teaching, exhorting or defending, planning or
encouraging, as of simply letting life follow its course. Once
sprung from its source, water carves out a river bed without any force other than its own. Its own force does the
job. In the same way the accompanist's role is extremely
simple: to let God's life follow its course in the other person. From the outset, he can thus welcome this other person with an intrinsic optimism. This brother or sister bears
within himself or herself an irresistible dynamism, so irresistible that it does not even need another person to
unfold. From time to time, it will doubtless be necessary
to neutralize some counter-force, to remove some interference which confuses the issue, as one would remove a
stone that had blocked up a water source. Most of the
time, this will be enough. Life propagates all by itself. For

life, there is nothing more natural, nothing less sophisti-
cated than sowing, propagating, and bearing fruit.

Let us take one more step towards understanding this
life force at work in each one of us by situating it at the
deepest, most intimate part of ourselves, at the source of
our being, where it merges with what recent literature
calls our 'interiority'. What does this mean? We could de-
fine it this way: a human being's interiority is that metaphysical place within him where, at every moment, God
touches him with his creative hand. In this place, God
ceaselessly creates 'man' and holds him in being. This activity of God, at the source of human being—and who 'is'
the source of human being—is intense and continuous. It
is even eternal, in one sense, because it is assured of eternity. If God decided the unthinkable—to withdraw his
hand and let him go—the human being would return at
that very instant to nothingness. The byzantine authors
called this place 'the place of God' in man (*ho topos tou
Theou*). It is like a secret 'metaphysical' sanctuary, that is to
say, beyond all physical or biological influences,
'metapsychical', too, beyond any psychological grasp, a
place where man is touched by God at each moment, even
though , at least under normal circumstances, this touch
is totally beyond human consciousness and superficial sensitivity.

To gain access to his fully developed humanity, something of this place of God within will need to manifest
itself to human consciousness, to be progressively integrated with it. The dialogue of spiritual accompaniment is
the place most conducive to giving such an event some
chance of occurring. In fact, this does not depend on our
efforts at all, nor on any technique of meditation or con-
centration. We can contribute very little, perhaps some
extremely simple discplines which favor asceticism and
create within us the space through which we may more
easily slip over into our interiority at the appropriate time.
It is not so much progress to be made or a distance to be

covered as suffering, undergoing, letting happen, letting things come to the surface. We must instead learn to let go a number of things, to stop many movements, to relax, abandon ourselves and even to lose our footing, to let ourselves sink into this deep reality in our heart, where Christ and the Spirit come to meet us. It is not that we go to meet them; they set out a long time ago to meet us. The important thing is not to miss their arrival, to be waiting at exactly the right place, the only place where the meeting can happen.

Specifically, one of the most important tasks of spiritual accompaniment will be teaching the brother/sister to remain exactly at the right place, available and dedicated to an untiring and interminable wait. God is always very close to us, not only close to, but within us, at the heart of ourselves, at the heart of our heart. We are the ones who are elsewhere, and sometimes very far away, even as we look all the while for God in places where it will always be far more difficult to meet him. Saint Augustine complained about this when, looking back over his life, he said: 'Late have I loved you . . ., for a long time I sought you outside of me, when you were near me, within me, *intimior intimo meo.*' [1]   And John Ruusbroec similarly, remarked that the love of Father and Son 'comes to us from the interior towards the exterior'.[2] Why watch the horizon so carefully, when it is on the landscape of the interior life that God will finally appear?

In one of his last works, Thomas Merton desscribed the mystic which—according to him—the accomplished monk should be, as a being who has finally arrived at the state of being *fully born*. The image sums up well, as in shorthand, everything we have said until now. Merton adds that this is the goal of what he calls—in a daring expression to which we can to some degree subscribe— the 'monastic

1. *Confessions,* 10.27.
2. *The Spiritual Espousals,* 2.58.

therapy', so long as nothing is opposed to its action and fruits. Following his example, we could just as well call it 'evangelical therapy'. The goal of such therapy is to allow the human person to accede to his full birth, the integration of the fullness of his humanity. 'The man who is fully born', writes Merton, 'possesses a total interior experience of his life. He grasps this fully and integrally from his interior core.'[3] Spiritual accompaniment deals mainly with the 'interior core'. But how can we discern it? How reach it? How learn to live from it? As soon as someone reaches the interior core which is his real self, he easily, as if naturally, detaches himself from his superficial self, without useless suffering, because he feels that he has reached a hitherto unknown fullness which can change his life.

This true self is part of a universal self shared by all his brothers and sisters. This is the reason why mystics and truly spiritual persons always seem universal. By reaching the most intimate depths of their redeemed being, they have touched an element beyond themselves which links them to the whole cosmos, which is also waiting for redemption, for an element which leads to God. They sense that they are intimately part of the new world as children of God and brothers of all other men. In Christ, they have become whole and universal 'man', an experience through which they reach their full identity, infinitely more fulfilling than all that is limited by their restricted self. They feel in communion with everyone, they experience the joy and suffering of everyone, and yet remain completely free from everything. Such persons have reached the ultimate freedom in which christian experience recognizes the freedom of the Spirit.

A discovery of interiority like this will necessarily be reflected in a person's behavior. This is how we can discern with some assurance whether the discovery of inte-

---

3. Thomas Merton, 'Rebirth and the New Man in Christianity', *Cistercian Studies [Quarterly]* 4 (1978) 289f.

riority has really taken place. In everything he says or undertakes, such a person is no longer completely like other people. He acts from an attentiveness turned inward, from listening to his own interiority. This is verified especially in the case of spiritual accompaniment. Since he is 'plugged in', so to speak, to the movements of his own interior life, he easily discerns the traces of this life in others. Instinctively he senses what is true and authentic, because it is welling up from within, and what is a superficial expression of more or less narcissistic desires. He no longer lets himself be led by generosity or the flexing of his will, nor even by reason or good principles. Not that he scorns all these or chooses not to want to take it into account, but because now all these instruments, as valuable as they are, are beside the point. His attitudes, choices and initiatives spring from within. Consequently, everything in him is entirely spontaneous and free, because everything emanates from love, according to its deepest reality. In French there is an expression which perfectly describes this activity born of deep freedom: something is said to 'flow from the source'. The image well expresses what it means to say. The source is interiority in the depth of each human being, at the heart of his heart: the Holy Spirit. To say of someone that humility 'flows from his source' is surely the highest compliment. There are two kinds of humility, Saint Bernard used to say. The first kind is cold, because it is the fruit of reason and exterior constraint, 'virtuous' in a questionable sense. The other, the kind which 'flows from the source', Bernard calls warm, because it springs from the deepest part of our being, as a fruit of the Holy Spirit.[4]

This passage from generous, virtuous conduct which is still constrained and stilted, to a conduct which is free and spontaneous, the fruit of the Spirit, has often been described by spiritual authors as a decisive step in spiritual

---

4. *Sermon 42.6 on the Song of Songs.*

growth. To give but a single example—the most classic one—let us recall a famous passage of the Rule of Saint Benedict, which all western monks and nuns know by heart. It comes at the conclusion of the chapter on humility:

> Having climbed all these degrees of humil-
> ity, the monk will soon reach that love of
> God which is perfect and casts out fear. By
> this love, all that previously he had observed
> not without fear, he will begin to observe
> without any effort *(sine labore!)*, no longer
> out of fear of hell, but out of love for Christ,
> familiarity in well-doing and delight in vir-
> tue *(RB 7)*.

Having reached the end of his journey, the monk has found within himself delight in virtue, *delectatio virtutum*. Hence-forth, he 'desires' this 'virtue'. It attracts and fascinates him. It supplants and even fulfills all his other desires. He rests in it as in his joy, just as he rests in the love of Christ. And this is why all spiritual activity becomes natural to him'–*velut naturaliter*–it flows from its source in him.

Such a description of the goal of spiritual accompani-ment may seem idyllic and unreal. It is—because no one here below has ever 'arrived' once and for all. The passage from the first step to the second is always somewhat par-tial and temporary. Moreover, the path is never perfectly straight. There are steps forward and backward, highs and lows. This is the rhythm of life here below, and the rhythm of all spiritual life. A certain ambiguity necessarily re-mains connected to our passage here. We will always 'still' be at the first stage, and on the other hand, we will 'al-ready' experience something of the next stage. We have one foot in the first stage and another in the second. We will never be entirely in the second stage, having in all fullness become new creatures. As Saint John Cassian re-marks in his *Conferences,* many Christians—and even

monks—still live partially in the Old Testament, under the
Old Law of fear and observances. Only progressively do
they pass into the New Testament regime, into the new
Law and freedom in the Spirit.[5] This remark is valuable
for our purpose. The role of spiritual accompaniment is
precisely helping and carefully supervising this passage
from the Law of constraint and fear to the Law of freedom in the Spirit, and this is at the heart of christian experience, which will always include a minimum of rites,
prescriptions and even 'commandments'; commandments
which no longer have any meaning other than leading
the believer progressively towards the full freedom of love.
This has not always been the case, we must concede, and
is not always the case even today.

Spending a little time on this deep reality, which constitutes in us the main object of spiritual accompaniment,
has been useful. Now that we have described it, we can
tackle the question of recourse to new methods and instruments offered to us today by what we call the human
sciences. Once we have recognized the absolute primacy
of the Spirit's life within us, it becomes possible to use
these sciences as objectively as possible and to the degree
to which they can be useful to us. No one seems able to
deny that they can be very useful, along with all the in-
sights required to prevent running the risk of getting
bogged down to the point of losing our bearings. For this,
it was important to see how only awareness of the Spirit's
life in us can put us on the road to knowing our own self
and our true destiny. Such knowledge implies an openness to obeying the Spirit's outpouring, the most intimate
law of our being, so that, having become perfectly free,
we can become the persons we are called to be. Of this
process of discovery and growth, the sciences we call 'human sciences' are the humble servant.

Before we close this chapter, here are some useful clari-

5. *Conference,* 21.31ff.

fications of vocabulary. To replace the once well-known phrase 'spiritual direction' the phrase 'spiritual accompaniment' has found favor with spiritual writers of the past several decades. The expression seems to have originated in Protestant circles to refer to the ministry of listening and being with the terminally ill. This is an extremely important time in a person's life, when he is facing the unknown, death, and the perspective of the next life. It creates a situation very uncomfortable for anyone, and as uncomfortable for those who are responsible for helping others at this time. Everyone faces the same unknown, which in some sense is doubly unknown by those who help from the outside and who cannot understand except at second hand. As someone has written:

> Accompanying indicates here a certain attitude towards the other. It is not to impose an itinerary on him, or even to know the direction he will take, but to walk beside him. In this realm, where a person learns to let go of life, this can only be a discreet help with paradoxical cries that must be decoded. To open oneself in this way to the unknown of what another is living, makes one vulnerable to the wounds inflicted by the relationship with death and the dying person himself.[6]

Death invokes the image of birth. It causes us to be born to the other life. Just as accompanying the terminally ill opens us to the birth which is death, so spiritual accompaniment opens us to new birth. It is helping someone be born to himself, to his true self, beyond his wounds and resistance. The accompanist accompanies, that is, walks

6. Léo Scherer, 'Si personne ne me guide... L'accompagnement spirituel', *Vie Chrétienne*, Supplement 328, p. 6.

beside someone on the same path. The accompanist indicates obstacles and pushes them aside. It is not for him to
precede nor to follow. His own personal path is often not
comparable to that of the person he accompanies. Each
path is very unique.

It is obvious that other words could be used instead of
accompanist: 'guide', 'master', 'director', 'father'/'mother',
and such corresponding counterparts as 'disciple',
'directee', 'son'/'daughter', even if some of these words
sound old-fashioned today. Each of these terms has a share
of truth, but none of them completely describes the content of the experience. The author quoted above continues:

> Perhaps this difficulty leads us to the es-
> sential truth. Christ, sent by the Father is
> the 'way, the truth and the life'. In an as-
> tonishing way, he accepted to become Mas-
> ter to make disciples, then he drew back to
> show the way and disappear, so that in their
> turn the disciples could become apostles and
> make disciples.

Beyond all doubt it is 'Christ in us, our hope of glory',
who is the essential object of spiritual accompaniment,
who is at the same time the only true accompanist. The
early christian community was already aware of this. No
doubt that is the reason it wanted to preserve a famous
saying which it placed in Jesus' mouth: 'Call no one Father; you have only one Father. Call no one Master; you
have only one Master: the Christ' *(Mt 23:8)*.

The Relationship between the Accompanist & the Person Accompanied 3

AS WE HAVE JUST SAID, we are not alone nor are we left to ourselves once we are granted an awareness of our interiority. It so sweeps over the person who experiences it that at the same moment he discovers what links him to all other human beings. In fact, because interiority is the life of God within us, it infinitely transcends each one of us, our age, our characteristics, the times in which we live, our culture. It constitutes a transpersonal reality which is also transhistoric. It is our share in eternity; by it we are in contact with all humanity and the universe. Here we have the basic condition for any spiritual accompaniment, because spiritual accompaniment is possible and effective only from communion around a shared interiority. In both persons, this accompaniment is able to open a path towards their deepest self, their true self in God. And this is so not because of what they do or say, but simply by what they are. As by a secret contagion or a very subtle osmosis, true life always irresistibly seeks to flow over to the partner.

Varied relationships

Before turning our attention to what happens at the heart of this kind of relationship, it may be important to point out that it happens differently in different cases. The variations in vocabulary used to speak of it already attest to this. When the relationship is particularly strong, the elders did not hesitate to speak of a true spiritual 'fatherhood'. This is still the language used in the Eastern Churches. We shall see in what sense and under which

45

conditions such vocabulary can be perfectly adequate. But it is evident that not all accompaniment relationships are that deep and are still not without value. On the contrary. This is why it is useful to distinguish several levels of depth, if you will, in the accompaniment relationship, each having its own importance. We shall distinguish in turn, without exaggerating the range of the terms we chose , a simple 'dialogue of accompaniment', 'spiritual pedagogy', then 'spiritual fatherhood' in the strict sense of the word. A brief description will suffice to introduce them.

The 'dialogue of accompaniment' surely represents the most frequent type. It is formed progressively, sometimes without really being noticed. A certain intimacy is progressively established with a neighbor who has certain qualities which are appreciated: a capacity for welcome, gift of sympathy, experience, prudence, spirit of faith. We feel at home with this person, and able to share things which we don't share with everyone. The frequency of exchanges varies according to stages and needs. It will spontaneously increase at times of crisis or when important decisions need to be made.

The person chosen may be a nearby priest, a confessor, a colleague or a friend. Sometimes the service rendered is reciprocal. Such a relationship is above all fraternal and friendly. It is woven and lived on equal terms. In religious life, superiors are not excluded from this role, but they are not necessarily the best placed to exercise such a ministry. Their 'fatherhood' or 'motherhood' is exercised first over the whole group, without excluding—it goes without saying—stronger personal relationships. In any case, such a relationship must remain perfectly free and spontaneous. It can never be imposed.

Despite its apparent simplicity, this bond deserves to be taken seriously, because eventually it may become deep, but must not be long-term or exclusive. It will easily vary according to circumstances. When circumstances change, a confidant of the same caliber can easily be chosen in the new surroundings. Several of these bonds can even coexist at the same time without rivalry or mutual harm. The simple dialogue of accompaniment ignores the unique and exclusive character–'once and for all'–which is decisive for spiritual fatherhood. It is even in its best interest to ignore it.

It is obvious that the great number of those who seek help, even among religious, will experience only this bond of accompaniment: a confidant, more or less a friend, with whom from time to time they will have a somewhat intimate exchange. As simple as it is and perhaps at first sight not deep, such a relationship should not be overlooked. On the contrary, every time two believers are gathered together, the Lord is present among them, with his Spirit, and something of the grace of accompaniment is really shared.

The case of 'spiritual pedagogy' is more specific, but far less common. As the chosen term indicates, it supposes a 'pedagogue', an educator or formation guide, as well as a situation in which a subject needs to be prepared or formed in view of a very concrete goal. This may be a delicate hurdle to get over, a particularly troubling crisis to go through, a new stage of growth, or simply the will of God to be discerned at the time of an important decision.

Specific examples would be the novitiate or a thirty day ignatian retreat or a retreat for the purpose of making a special decision. In all these cases, the relationship of accompaniment is circumscribed within a restricted period of time during which a particular, well-tried method will be implemented intensively, usually for a specific objective: preparing for a commitment, making a choice, accepting a trial, confronting a decisive turning-point in life.

This time, at least in most cases, the one accompanying is not chosen by the subject himself. He is designated by someone else. If a choice is allowed, it is restricted and limited to a list of candidates who are considered competent, because the master here cannot be just anyone. He must be a professional, prepared for this particular task, who will act according to a tested method in which he has acquired experience and a certain skill, for he has only a limited time in which to lead the subject to take a decisive step. This is also why he will usually be the only one, and his intervention must have priority over that of other confidants or that of a community. Also, the relationship formed between him and the person accompanied will tend to reflect that which exists between a master and a disciple.

Finally, there is 'spiritual fatherhood' / 'spiritual motherhood' in the strict sense, the sense in which our brothers in the Eastern Churches usually understand it. There it is held in very great honor, and rightly so. This is also— under a sometimes somewhat idealized form—what western Christians think back to with nostalgia these days, once they become aware again of their need to be accompanied. They are both right and wrong at the same time. They are right because 'spiritual fatherhood' is a reality which still exists in the heart of the Church, but they would be wrong hastily and without reflection to use a vocabulary which can be open to illusion. This relationship exists—as long Tradition attests—but as a relatively rare and properly inimitable charism. This charism does not come to the spiritual 'father' from his ability or experience. It comes from God as an unexpected gift and as the revelation of God's own fatherhood.

'Spiritual fatherhood' will be revealed within preexisting relationships—how could it be otherwise?—between two friends, novice master and novice, superior and brother. But it does not come from this relationship. No relationship or authority ever justify such a grace. It is not, for example, because someone has been appointed novice master that this grace is due in any way. It is of another order and always a free gift. This is why no one must ever suppose or presume it. The risk is not negligible, because the relationship of spiritual fatherhood leads to such transparency of heart, it confers such spiritual authority, although accepted in the liberty of love, that any gratuitous presumption might lead to disaster. Sometimes a person exercises it without being aware of it. A person may have marked someone for life without ever being aware of it. It is the other who knows—but not always—because it is first of all his faith which has been fulfilled.

Because of what it is, such a relationship is unique and exclusive of any other which might be of the same quality. For ever, one will have had only one father. This is the fruit by which we recognize that the relationship was true. One should never expect it to be perpetuated or reproduced in the same way. That would be completely useless if the relationship had really been the occasion of a spiritual birth, a decisive passage towards life in God. When the day comes that the 'father' disappears from the scene, there will be no need to look for another. The son will have to grieve for him, as every son must grieve for his father, and start again, living now with his memory, his secret love, but above all with that anointing of the Spirit which the father was the first to help him discover at the deepest part of his heart; from now on the Spirit will 'teach him everything' *(1 Jn 2:27)* and will be all he needs.

In this specific form called 'spiritual fatherhood' in the strict sense, accompaniment is not necessary to everyone. The fatherhood of God is demonstrated in many ways in the life of each believer, but not necessarily in this typical and exemplary form. One must not regret or desperately seek at any cost to find the 'father' who has not yet been found. Much less must anyone believe that he is personally invested with this role towards someone else, not even, and especially not, his best friends. Mainly here, where it would only by way of exception correspond to the lived reality, it is appropriate to be slow to believe and spontaneously reticent to use the vocabulary of spiritual fatherhood or sonship.

A true accompaniment can be exercised in many other ways, and we may believe that something of this exceptional charism is obscurely present in all relationships among believers. We are perhaps all called to be a bit of a father or mother to a number of brothers and sisters-without seeking and often knowing it, as we said. In the light of this 'fatherly' grace, analogously, many aspects of our everyday humbler fraternal relationships can be seen in a new light. All no doubt carry something of this grace which God has decided to give us through our brothers and sisters.

AT THE HEART OF A HUMAN RELATIONSHIP

Now let us take a closer look at the bond which will be woven between two people who are face to face: the one who asks to be accompanied and the one who does the accompanying. Right away we are at the heart of a human relationship which is suddenly about to take on a new importance. Within this relationship a road will be traveled. In a certain sense, we could say that spiritual accompaniment is identified with this relationship and even that this is its most immediate object. What happens to both persons within this relationship will allow something to happen to each of them.

There are different kinds of human relationships. We may think that the relationship of accompaniment constitutes not only a very particular, but also a privileged, human relationship. Here are two human beings who are present to each other, called to walk along together for a while. Between them something is going to happen, an event will take place. An event in the strongest sense of the word, it will be much more than sharing knowledge or giving advice. Someone who just wants to know is seeking to satisfy his intellectual curiosity. Someone who just wants to do what is right wants to be in harmony with the law or his conscience. This is enough for him, nothing else is expected. The request of someone seeking an accompanist goes way beyond this, even if he is not able to explain it clearly at the beginning. He is soliciting more than knowledge or even wisdom. He aspires to a deeper life, not so much the life of the person whom he approaches, but his own life, the life which is still sleeping in the depths of his heart. In other words, he is seeking to be born, or reborn, at a more intimate level of his being, and he has vaguely sensed that the person to whom he goes can help him bring this life to birth in him.

In a case of spiritual accompaniment, as we have seen, the deep life aimed at is that of the Holy Spirit in person, the Spirit who must reveal himself in the other. This is the event to which he aspires more or less unwittingly. By associating with the specific person whom he has chosen as guide, he hopes that a spark of life will shoot out between them, from the guide to him, at the very heart of the relationship between them. Again, not just any life, but the light and strength of the Spirit.

To say that this is a spiritual event—in the past we would have called it a supernatural event—does not imply that such an event can be divorced in any way from the concrete human relationship which unites these two persons. On the contrary. For the first time we are meeting a question which will often recur in one form or another in the following pages. What is the relationship between natural and supernatural at the heart of spiritual accompaniment? Is it possible precisely to distinguish elements which are exclusively of the order of nature and other elements which are only spiritual and which would therefore be privileged over the first elements? For the moment, let us underline the impossibility of hoping for such a 'discernment' or separation. In any human relationship, we can never say: 'Until this point this relationship is natural; from this other point on, it becomes spiritual'. A father who loves his son, a friend who loves a friend, loves him always more or less in the same way, with the same affective density or quality. The 'spiritual' character of the relationship is not added on outside the natural character. It is present everywhere at the very heart of it in the form of a positive orientation to the meaning of a deepened life. All that is spiritual is thus incarnated in the natural. The life of the Spirit is never superimposed on our psychology; it is one with it. Let us remember the saying of Charles Péguy, shocking in his day: 'The carnal itself is spiritual'.

This human relationship, with its characteristics and opportunities and also its resistance and pitfalls, with all its possibilities, exists to serve the spiritual event anticipated at the heart of the relationship of accompaniment. Therefore, it is important to take pains with the quality of this relationship, and to do this, it is necessary to know its pitfalls, the better to avoid them. This concerns the quality of the relationship, not its quantity, the frequency of contact, the number of letters or their length, the length of time spent talking, to cite only the most basic kind of traps in which a relationship of accompaniment always risks being snared. It is even certain that too frequent meetings may even in some circumstances prevent the event and maintain the two partners in a completely ineffective *status quo*.

The terminology used by the elders to speak of the relationship of spiritual accompaniment shows very well the extent to which they considered it one of the privileged forms of human relationship. Kierkegaard said that a spiritual guide was 'more than a friend'. When Dante painted the idealized portrait of the guide in the traits of Virgil, Beatrice and finally Saint Bernard, he said of Virgil that he was 'more than a father'. In the buddhist vocabulary, the term 'lama' means 'incomparable mother'. And we know that *kaloïros,* the name given by the greek monks to their elders, means 'beautiful old man', a term which suggests both the summit of wisdom and tenderness.

'More than a friend', 'more than a father', 'incomparable mother'—these terms which evoke images with affective overtones, speak for themselves. They allude to what must be, at the heart of the relationship, the quality of the person accompanying, contact with whom lets life spring up and be transmitted. We will speak about this later, but already we may give it a more specific name. This quality in the relationship is called love, but love in the strongest sense of the word—we might even be tempted to say 'more than love'— *agapè*. The person accompanying is among us completely made in the image of God and his Son. On the face of a man or a woman, through his or her words and actions, something of the love of God shows through. The love of God, in the relationship we are describing, designates at one and same time great tenderness and sweetness coupled with great strength and firmness. This is very important. In real life, it can take extraordinarily simple forms. It can be something very small: a silence, a glance, a small gesture, a simple word of acquiescence, which and astounds and transforms. Suddenly, a depth hitherto unimagined opens up in the person accompanied. It is as if he recognizes himself, identifies himself, as if afterwards, unexpectedly, he knows who he really is. To use a biblical term, it is as if a new name were revealed to him, one that he immediately senses is his true name, for in it he recognizes himself; a name which is known only to him and the one who enunciated it for him. This is a kind of rebirth, a birth to the only true life. This is probably due to the violence of this realization, very concretely experienced, that the very first christian generations in the days of Saint Paul, and after him monastic communities, have not hesitated to introduce the vocabulary of fatherhood and motherhood, and this despite a very explicit warning in the Gospels against it. In fact, up to a certain point this vocabulary is true. Modern psychology, using many concrete experiences, teaches us that biological fatherhood is not enough if fatherhood is not concretely exercised during the very first years of life; just as psychological fatherhood later on can effectively fill gaps in upbringing going back to a person's childhood. This is true only on the condition that this substitute upbringing and this foster fatherhood, as it were, can be correctly exercised, that is, in increasing the autonomy of the person concerned.

The love which reveals itself at the heart of the relationship of accompaniment is only another name for the deep life of the Holy Spirit which is the basis of the relationship and the sharing between the one accompanying and the one accompanied. Similarly, this love is identified with the spiritual health and human development which are the goal of all accompaniment. The basis of psychological balance is also found in the capacity truly to love. We are healthy, and if necessary we can do without accompaniment, to the degree to which we are able to love truly, that is unconditionally, as God loves. Love is the capacity for going out of oneself towards the other without expecting return to oneself, the capacity to give oneself to the other without expecting anything in exchange. Through love, we affirm the other while being affirmed ourselves, but without seeking this. In love, we give without taking because we find ourselves by losing ourselves.

How does one become a spiritual accompanist? Who is called to become one? How is this bond, which brings two persons ever closer in such an intimate way, concretely created? By asking this question, we leave aside any objective conditions which often favor such a relationship—for example, the case of someone who may be given an explicit ministry or in obedience be asked to take it on . The most obvious example is the novice master or novice mistress, named to this service by a superior. One can also prepare professionally, so to speak, to exercise such a role by specialized studies or sessions organized for this purpose, all of which are obviously perfectly legitimate. However, all this does not infallibly guarantee that such a bond will really be created, nor that it will be fruitful. In fact, in the concrete circumstances of life other conditions will come into play, which are not easy to analyze since many facets are blended and intertwined. Again, we are faced with the question which has already come up and which–let us say right away–must remain for a long time without a satisfactory answer: what is the respective weight of the psychological aptitudes and spiritual quality in one who is called to accompany?

Let us clarify first that no one can take such a function upon himself or presume on his capabilities in this regard. On his door or business card, someone can write: 'Physiotherapist' or 'Psychoanalyst'. No one can write 'Spiritual father' or 'Spiritual accompanist'. The two types of assistance do not belong to the same order. Spiritual Fatherhood is not a profession, the exercise of which can be guaranteed by a diploma. Let us repeat: no one can set himself up as anyone's spiritual accompanist or claim the title recklessly. Most of the time the opposite will happen, and it is important to repeat this: it is not the father who chooses his son, it is the son who discovers his father. It is not for the one accompanying to say to anyone: 'You will be my disciple!' It is the disciple who will discern his Master. This is an absolute rule which seems to allow no exception.

Here the reader may raise an objection: the process which has just been described cannot be verified when the accompaniment is exercised as a ministry officially assigned by a superior authority—as, among other examples, in the case of the novice master or novice mistress to which we alluded. Indeed, these persons have not chosen their novices, and it is also true that the novices generally have not had the opportunity to choose their novice guardian. The novices are imposed on the master and vice versa. So what? As we have already said: in a novitiate, the ministry of accompaniment exercised by the novice master/mistress is a particular type of ministry— extremely important, it goes without saying—but with well defined limits and a very specific goal. In most cases, it does not necessarily imply, and certainly not at the beginning, spiritual accompaniment in the strong sense of which we are speaking now. We need only recall here what has been said above about the analogical character of accompaniment, the principal form and several derived forms which are often more frequent. Each has its own effectiveness. It follows that the dialogue between the novice master and the novice, far from being a criterion for objection, is very close to what will now follow. This form of dialogue is almost exactly the same as spiritual accompaniment—the same issues and the same risks, yet with this limitation on one essential point: we must never presume that the brother has inwardly consented to the relationship becoming any deeper than the objective relationship between a master and his novices. In the terms of Canon Law, the external forum must not be confused with the internal forum, and the novice master/mistress is not authorized to enter the intimacy of a conscience without having been expressly invited.

It remains obvious that the dialogue between novice guardian and novice is the ideal ground where a relationship of accompaniment can begin and be formed. On the other hand, it is just as important that the novice recognizes and accept his accompanist as such. That the son is to awaken his father's fatherhood, and the disciple reveal the master is well-known.

The result is that, within the relationship of spiritual accompaniment, the attitude of the one accompanied is more important than the attitude of the one accompanying, who may well be taken completely by surprise. Many things may sometimes happen without, or almost without, his knowledge. It is the interior attitude of the one accompanied which is to be paramount and decisive. In the end, it is even the only thing required: an attitude of desire, waiting, and openness. This is what will awaken in his partner the guide and master who are still sleeping within him.

Underlining this essential condition for spiritual accompaniment is important in view of the complaint often heard: 'I cannot find a spiritual father' or 'There are no more spiritual fathers in the Church today'. Not that there is nothing objective which corresponds to such a complaint. Certainly the climate and certain conditions today do not encourage the awakening of this relationship. It remains true, however, that the essential precondition of accompaniment always comes from the person who sincerely seeks. He cannot help but find—if he himself is sufficiently ready. The hindu saying is true here: 'When the disciple is ready, the master appears'. We find a similar affirmation in a famous saying:

> A desert father asked another father: 'Why do monks today have no more words to give?' [in our terms: why are there no longer good spiritual fathers today?]
> Answer: 'Because the sons no longer know how to listen.'

The quality of seeking and listening in the end gives rise to an accompanist. Certain ancient authors referred to this as the quality of faith. This is the answer Dorotheus of Gaza gave to monks who were complaining that they had not found the spiritual father so long sought, one able to reveal the will of God to them:

> If anyone really in truth desires the will of God with all his heart, God never leaves him [to himself], but always guides him according to His will. If a man really sets his heart upon the will of God, [God] will enlighten a little child to tell that man what is His will. But if a man does not truly desire the will of God, even if he goes in search of a prophet, God will put into the

heart of the prophet a reply like the decep-
tion of his own heart.[1]

Once again, what counts is not the knowledge or the experience or the competence of the one accompanying,
but rather the profound surrender of the one who asks.

Even so, something preliminary is given to the two partners in the relationship: a premonition which the person
accompanied has vaguely sensed without being totally conscious of it. Between him and his future accompanist,
there exists a secret complicity, a subtle reciprocity. This
happens at a deep level of being, the true self of which we
spoke earlier. The key which gives us access to our intimate life is, of course, found within us, not within someone else, even if we do not know how to extricate this key
right away or how to use it. But something from outside—a word, a gesture, the depth of a relationship—will
have to touch us decisively to stir an harmonic, deep chord.
Essentially, this is what we expect of a companion, and at
the same time we have an obscure premonition that only
he and no other could give us that gesture or that word.
We expect his mystery to touch and unveil our own mystery, the mystery each person carries within and with
which, in the one who initiates us into this mystery, we
will then feel in harmony.

The profound mystery of the one accompanying and
the relationship he succeeds in establishing between himself and this mystery thus play a very important role in
the choice, even if these elements often remain impon-
derable and escape precise analysis. One does not know,
one senses. This allows us to think that we are somehow
destined to have this accompanist rather than another.
This is because what he will cause to come to the surface
in the heart of the person accompanied springs first from
his own heart. There is a mysterious harmony pre-estab-

1. Dorotheos of Gaza, *Instructions* 5.68; translation by Eric Wheeler,
Dorotheos of Gaza: Discourses and Sayings (CS 33:129).

lished between the two partners. As important as the gestures and words of the one accompanying are, this is why they have value only relative to his deepest being. Of themselves, they can be insignificant or purely symbolic. But it is important that they transmit an inner key which will give access to the inner life. They must open the way to the 'Interior Master', as Saint Augustine called what in spiritual accompaniment can only be the Holy Spirit in person, the Spirit who is infallibly granted to us and remains present to us inwardly and in advance of any spiritual desire or commitment on our part. At the heart of accompaniment, the ideal would be for the 'Exterior Master' to become, as it were, one with the Interior Master, until he is able to step aside totally. This ideal is never perfectly achieved because of the many ambiguities which stand in the way of dialogue, and even sometimes the pitfalls with which it is almost inevitably strewn.

Another image lets us specify the quality of this relationship, the one recommended by Socrates when he called his method 'maieutics', the coming to truth of a disciple led by the master. Maieutics, we know, is the term given the knowledge of a midwife who assists at the birth of a new life. She is not the one who gives life, she only helps it, facilitates its coming to full term. All life propagates naturally, of itself. The fetus generally has no need of outside help to come into the world. In most cases, however, the midwife's intervention, as discreet as it may be, is useful and even desirable. She supervises the procedure, foresees and anticipates obstacles, promotes certain stages. The spiritual accompanist's role is the same, analogously. He also assists at a birth: the coming into this world of a new creature in the Holy Spirit. This is a real birth or rebirth. The life of the Holy Spirit comes to the surface, rises from the depths of a person's being before saturating in turn all the layers of that human being, from the most inward to the most exterior. We pass progressively 'from the old man to the new man'. This unfolding of life happens very naturally. The life of the Spirit is powerful enough to make its way through human psychology and strengths. Strictly speaking, it does not need this exterior accompaniment. Yet this is not only useful, but even desirable, in most cases. The one accompanying can effectively supervise the process of the soul in labor, indicate an orientation, avoid pitfalls, go around obstacles. And perhaps even this is not saying enough, because accompaniment is, so to speak, the usual way, for it is almost always through a fraternal relationship that the life of the Spirit succeeds in propagating itself in us.

The person accompanied is not the only beneficiary, because the quality of the relationship of accompaniment engages both partners so strongly that advantages accrue to both at the same time. In most cases, what happens to one— usually first the one accompanied—speaks so forcefully to the freedom of the other—that is, the one accompanying—that he also is called to grow in an awareness of his interior reality. Both evolve together and the growth of the one necessitates and provokes the growth of the other. One of the most famous spiritual fathers of contemporary monasticism, Father Matta el-Meskin, of the coptic monastery of Saint Macarius in the desert of the Wadi-el-Natroun, speaking from his own experience, expresses it thus:

> What God has given me concerning the
> experience of souls so far surpasses what
> he has given me, that I feed on the crumbs
> which fall from the table which God has
> prepared for others through me.[2]

On several occasions we have had the opportunity of comparing the experience of spiritual accompaniment

---

2.   Quoted by Léo Scherer, 'Si personne ne me guide' [above, Chapter 2, note 6], p. 30.

with related realities either in other—especially eastern—religions or with the techniques and practices of the human sciences. The similarity between both paths of spiritual accompaniment is significant. Each supposes a relatively similar interior *ascesis*. It always deals with leaving our superficial being, our small self or our relative self, to advance into our deep being, our true Self which reveals itself successively by stages. Each of us bears within ourself, unconsciously, richness which can be glimpsed from time to time in symbolic form—for example, in our most serene and peaceful dreams. Life on earth is given to us precisely to give this treasure the opportunity of coming progressively to the surface of our being, of being integrated with our conscious life. Each human being is called in this way to enrich himself with his interior treasure in an unending progression, because the treasure in question is infinitely larger than any one of us within the confines of our personality and personal history. It is a universal treasure, destined for all. The Christian has no difficulty recognizing the very life of the Holy Spirit which he knows to be present in the heart of each human being.

Let us hypothesize that such a process of growth and integration were perhaps to end during a person's lifetime: such a person would be devitalized, become sterile and virtually dead. On the other hand, the secret of some older people who are said to have kept a surprisingly young heart is precisely this capacity to use every occasion, even those apparently the most annoying and negative, to allow new possibilities of inward life come to the surface. These 'old people' appear eternally young because they never stop enriching themselves from their interior, seemingly inexhaustible, treasure—as in truth it is. No matter in what new circumstance they find themselves, they are always able to make it their own and to draw experience from it, that is, always improve their inward treasure by contact with these circumstances, both for their own profit and that of others. This amazing flexibility towards life is the secret of their youthfulness. They are like a tree which each year sprouts new flowers and produces new fruits until death puts an end to the cycle. And the destiny of a tree which no longer bears fruit is the same as a soul whose growth is exhausted or has been irremediably impeded. Decline sets in, the sense of our presence here below is at the same time filled with possibilities extended and void of completion. Our life on earth, cut off from the great process of life we described, loses its meaning. There is nothing for any being so marked to do but to 'cross to the other side', that is, to go through death. Because it is only through death, after this new and ultimate passing, that the life of the Spirit within us can bear new fruits for eternity, fruits still utterly unforseeable today.

DIVINE LIFE AND HUMAN SCIENCES

Now let us say a few words about the relationship between the life of God within us and our concrete psychological makeup. We have already pointed out the impossibility of making a distinction between the psychological and spiritual quality of a relationship of accompaniment. These two dimensions are totally interlinked, even though they belong to different orders. We run into the same difficulty when we come to surprising or detecting the motions of the Spirit or the fruits of the Spirit in our own psychology or that of others. This is not surprising. It flows from what classical philosophy called the substantial and not accidental union of the soul and the body. Everything in the human person, incarnate spirit, is both spirit and flesh, and any separation between the two brings death, that is, passage to another metaphysical state. This assessment also flows, at an even deeper level, from the substantial union between the Word and human nature which took place at the Incarnation. The Word assumed all of man, in the totality of his humanity and thus of his psychology.

It follows that the divine life in which we participate by our incorporation into Christ at our baptism cannot be isolated and detached from our psychology. Certainly, this is not to be identified purely and simply with our psychology, but up to a point which is hard to pinpoint more precisely, it cannot be completely detached from it. The surgeon while operating is perfectly able to distinguish one organ from another, to discern between a nerve and a vein, for instance. But his scalpel can never isolate his patient's soul, even if he were to die on the operating table. Similarly, there is no spiritual surgery which could delimit exactly what is purely psychological and what is exclusively supernatural. The supernatural or the spiritual are as such completely beyond the competence not only of the surgeon but also of the psychiatrist and the psychoanalyst. Any psychologist who, by virtue of his professional qualifications, believed he was authorized to pronounce a moral or spiritual judgment would at that point simply leave the field of his competence. Although it is important that each person remain within his own field and respect those of others, it is no longer possible to practice spiritual accompaniment as if psychology did not exist, as if research in this field did not lead to certain accepted facts which can no longer reasonably be questioned. Few persons today would doubt the ability of the psychological sciences to bring substantial help, so long as each remains in his own field.

If we cannot separate the life of the Spirit and psychology in any particular person, this is because the life of the Spirit in him necessarily leans on his psychology, that is, leans very concretely on both the positive and the negative aspects of this psychology—to be more specific, even on the 'negative' aspects of this psychology. This is important, because it is relatively easy for us to discern the action of God in the positive and consequently reassuring aspects of human psychology, but it is generally much more difficult for us to discern this by the negative aspects which are more threatening to us and everyone else. God is at work in both, and an assessment of spiritual discernment must always take into account the positive and negative aspects of a psychology.

Let us take a very concrete example, one of the most frequent: discerning a religious vocation. No one has to be a novice master or a psychologist to admit without difficulty that the ideal candidate for religious life, someone who presents only positive qualities, does not exist. Fortunately! But we can say more: in the discernment of a vocation, what is important are not the positive qualities of a personality, its negative aspects, or rather the way in which these negative aspects are lived out relative to a possible vocation. This is because—and this is extremely important—if there is indeed a vocation from God, this vocation will lean just as much on the negative aspects of the candidate's psychology as on the positive. In the same way, the candidate may perhaps one day freely choose to answer this call, taking into account the positive and negative aspects of his personality.

We can go even further. When there is a real vocation, this does not necessarily imply that the positive spiritual growth of the subject will at length bring about a psychological improvement or even a cure. Such growth is possible, and sometimes it really happens, but it is not necessary and it is in no way a decisive criterion of vocation—that is, if there were to be no psychological improvement, it would mean that one had been mistaken about the vocation. Psychological therapy and spiritual healing sometimes go together, or they can sometimes occur simultaneously, but they are never totally synonymous. In certain cases—fortunately quite frequently—a positive spiritual development causes psychological elements which had been more or less disrupted to go back to their proper place. And one might think that this is a real and highly estimable fruit of the action of the Holy Spirit. But this fruit remains a free gift. It is not guaranteed in advance nor is it indispensable, and in no case should it be treated as an infallible criterion of the presence or absence of a spiritual fruit, because the Holy Spirit is perfectly able to create such fruit through a blocked or seriously disturbed psychological condition. The important thing to discern is always the way in which the subject accepts and passes through the trial. Discernment here aims to see measure to which the subject is interiorly attuned to what the Holy Spirit reveals to him at the heart of this distress, as trying as it may be. The Holy Spirit is at work everywhere and expects from us only one thing: that we pay attention to his movement, and that we agree to yield to it, to let ourselves be acted upon by him. 'Those who let themselves be led by the Spirit are truly sons of God' (Rm 8:14). 'Everything works together for good for those who love God' (Rm 8:28). To these words of Saint Paul, the twelfth-century author of a work which passed under Saint Augustine's name had the audacity to add *etiam peccata*, even sins![3] All the more reason to include psychological malformations, frustrations, and blocks.

Of course, what we have just said should not make us naive when we must discern the reality of any vocation. There are other important criteria besides that which allows us to see that a candidate is perfectly attuned to the life of the Spirit within him, despite his handicap. The most important criterion will always be God's call, insofar as this can be identified through the free choice of the subject who acquiesces to a grace clearly recognized. It is at this very point that discernment becomes difficult. It would be more reassuring if God called to christian life only persons with a perfectly balanced psychological makeup. But evidently this is not his good pleasure. And the fact that it pleases him sometimes to call to authentic love and true holiness persons whose psychology is very damaged is only

3.   See Ernest Dutoit, *Tout saint Augustin* (Fribourg, Switzerland, 1988) 173-174. The same doctrine is found clearly formulated by Saint Augustine in *De correptione et gratia,* 24.

the expression of his merciful plan throughout history, as the Gospel tells us: he chooses the poor, he raises the humble.

Transference   4

EFORE APPROACHING the subject of spiritual dialogue more concretely, it may be appropriate to say a few words about what inevitably constitutes the support of spiritual dialogue, that is, the relationship and, more specifically, the transference in which the two partners in the relationship are inevitably engaged, whether they like it or not. This will require a little detour through certain data psychology generally accepted by everyone today. A little familiarity with these can save us many deceptions.

Thanks to the process of psychoanalytic treatment, and particularly to the attentive analysis of the bonds formed between the analyst and his client, we know more today about the relational phenomenon to which Freud gave the name 'transference'. Freud,in fact, noticed—very accurately—that his clients had the habit of transferring on to him, their analyst, the feelings they had in the past felt towards their parents. This mixture of positive and negative feelings had repercussions in their adult life and habitually colored their attitude towards all forms of authority, going so far as to spread like an oil stain over their whole life: work relationships, friendships, family relationships with spouse and children and, we can add, when they are believers, in their relationship with God. Each person, in his relationships with others, he concluded, has a tendency ceaselessly to repeat a certain scenario, most often solidly padlocked. This scenario was generally set up in early childhood with the means then available for facing the suffering and frustrations which at the time would have been psychologically unbearable.

Freud's genius was to understand right away the therapeutic benefit he could draw from this clinical observation. If the original scenario infallibly reproduced itself in the analyst-client relationship—and in a particularly acute way, as if pushed to its limit—why not take advantage of it to go back in the history of the scenario, hitherto locked, and make it evolve in a positive way. For this, he thought, it would be necessary, not to refuse the transfer or defend himself against it, but to enter into it, to agree to play a role, but not just any role. If, as Jacques Lacan maintained, transference is the 'actualization of the reality of the unconscious', an opportunity was thus offered of having some grasp on the unconscious by trying first to identify it, and then attempting to give it new meaning and imprint on it a less traumatic orientation.

The analyst then welcomes the transfer and agrees to enter into the scenario and to play the role his client assigns him. Yet, as we have just said, in a very specific way. He cannot enter passively into the scenario or simply undergo it, trying to satisfy the client with some gratification to compensate for the frustrations experienced when the scenario was played out earlier. Neither can he let the impasses the patient encountered in his relationship with his parents repeat themselves indefinitely. Experience has shown that acting the transference out in this way only confirms and reinforces the scenario, without hope of evolution.

Transference is complicated by the fact that the client is not the only one to transfer and project his feelings. The analyst is also engaged in this and finds himself in turn enticed into his own scenario within his client's scenario, which from that time on involves the therapist's own frustrations and their tendency to satisfy themselves by compensations. To some degree the analyst suffers as much as his client from primitive frustrations and builds up an unconscious scenario to escape the sufferings they cause him. This means that his client's transfer onto him, whether positive or negative, touches him and affects him in his own more or less unconscious scenario, creating in him what Freud justly called the counter-transfer. Right away it becomes evident that the confrontation of these two transfers, the client's and the analyst's, will be delicate to manage, and that the happy outcome of such a confrontation will depend on several factors. The most important will be that the analyst himself be clear about his own scenario and frustrations. Otherwise the situation can rapidly become explosive or, at least, be of no therapeutic value.

In whatever way the analyst decides to be involved in the transfer, it is appropriate that he always do so in an adequately neutral and detached manner. What is important is not his own scenario but his client's. This does not mean that the analyst must deny himself any feelings at all. That would not only be impossible, but, more importantly, it would introduce into the relationship with his client a 'taboo' which could only have a harmful influence on the client's evolution. The analyst will thus peacefully welcome his own feelings, while being careful to manage them correctly: by accepting to want 'not to desire to be satisfied', which is very different from wanting 'not to desire purely and simply'. The rest of this account will specify what is meant by this formula. The reader will already have established that the present insistence on the attitude of the analyst towards counter-transfer implies a link between the therapeutic relationship in psychoanalysis and the relationship of spiritual accompaniment.

It would be pointless to say more at this time about proper conduct in a situation of transfer and counter-transfer. We will return to this topic when we describe more concretely the hazards of spiritual dialogue. Various schools of psychoanalysis differ, moreover, in their interpretation of the process of transference—a well-known fact—thus giving rise to sometimes contradictory therapeutic techniques. Although all agree in accepting the validity of Freud's fundamental insight, the concrete applications in therapy vary, sometimes widely. We may believe that each of them, to the degree it is based on methods verified by conclusive results, contains its share of truth, and would be able to complement other points of view. By trying to factor Freud's discovery into the way of living out a relationship of accompaniment, this author will very probably be led—without wanting and even perhaps without noticing it—to make a very specific application which will no doubt seem to deviate from some current freudian orthodoxy. We need only mention it honestly, without having here to debate further.

The reader may have the vague suspicion that we have exaggerated and given too large a place here to the aspect of transference in the relationship of accompaniment. Is doing this not looking at things in too natural a way, without adequately taking into account the absolute predominance of the action of the Spirit at the heart of this relationship? Does the whole art of spiritual accompaniment not consist in escaping the 'temptation' to transference, with all its ambiguity and complications? Would it not be enough simply to refuse this situation and try to neutralize its most irritating symptoms or even vigorously combat them, leaving the field open to the action of the Spirit? The objection is very important. It is even attractive. It was surely worth formulating.

A first answer consists in observing that the transfer is not at all a 'temptation' which one might escape. It is a fact, whether one wills it or not, whether one conceals it or not. We are tempted to recall the famous saying: 'A fact is more respectable than the Lord Mayor of London.' Of course, it is a fact which partly escapes consciousness, a fact which is partly unconscious. But everyone knows that psychological realities are much more to be feared and have only pernicious effects when they remain unconscious and someone avoids facing them. Transfer, however, is only very partially unconscious. A practiced eye can, relatively easily, detect it by certain signs which cannot deceive. To someone who has any experience of a relationship of accompaniment that is more than a simple moralistic briefing, transfer is simply obvious.

If the transfer is not a temptation but, on the contrary, a fact which cannot be ignored, concealing or fighting it would be pointless. Such an attitude would have the totally opposite effect. Concealing or fighting the transfer would be another way of taking it into account, and even a way of adopting the scenario of the person accompanied, while pretending to do the opposite. The relationship would be complicated and result in fixing the scenario even more firmly. In most cases the first result of combating the transfer is to add a new frustration to old ones, a new guilt to those that already weigh on the partner. They can only lead him to strengthen the unconscious defense mechanism he has built against such annoyances.

The embarrassment we feel in hearing about transference is normal and perfectly understandable. It seems to cast a suspicion on our best intentions. In any case, it seems to complicate radically and even compromise the ministry of accompaniment. It is not surprising that we experience an almost insurmountable reticence to take it into account and especially to enter into it and be committed to it. We can even experience a kind of threat which risks destabilizing us or uncovering in ourselves wounds that we may have suspected but had not yet had a chance to look at squarely. All this goes without saying, so true is it that, at least in principle and to a certain point, true accompaniment can only be done by one who has first made the journey as someone accompanied.

Accompanying another person can, moreover, more or less effectively remedy in part the deficiencies of the accompaniment a person has himself previously received, because for the person accompanying the situation of transfer is also first an opportunity and not a

risk. Managed correctly, it can finally force him positively to renounce his desires, teach him to want something without being granted it, by obliging him to step
aside constantly before the other person's growing freedom and autonomy. In short: it is an uncommon chance
to learn to love truly. It is well-known that in spiritual
accompaniment both partners benefit equally.

Transference, as important as it is, does not exhaust
the meanings of the relationship implied in the dialogue of accompaniment. Far from it, and this is important to note. Every relationship contains far more
than transfer and counter-transfer: a real possibility
is offered of contact in depth, in which the true self
of the one enters into communion with the true self
of the other. An english analyst, Fred Blum, has called
this possibility the 'third dimension' of every analytical
relationship. This third dimension, which is not unrelated
to Love or the life of God in the heart of each, contains the
creative power which transforms the relationship and effects healing.

The classic techniques of psychoanalysis seem to ignore
this third dimension. Many people remain at the stage of
transfer and counter-transfer, where the whole art of the
analyst consists in recognizing and welcoming the transfer, and then evading it. The neutrality of the analysis—
which for him is a form of love—sets him in a place where
the client's desire, distorted by the transfer, can no longer
reach him. The analyst remains obstinately out of reach,
constantly sidestepping to escape the grip of the other's
desire. Thus he sends the other person inexorably back to
himself and the progressive acceptance of his frustrations,
because, according to Freud's hypothesis, behind all desires there is a desire which is forever forbidden, and in
any case could never be fulfilled. Human wisdom, the only
wisdom possible in his eyes, consists then in accepting
this flaw which can never be repaired and in being reconciled to a lack which can never be remedied.

Reduced to this kind of teaching method, analytical therapy can certainly lead to a form of highly respectable human wisdom which is not without a certain evangelical resonance. Such a method seems, however, inadequate to account for all the values which are or could effectively be engaged in the relationship of accompaniment and with which monastic history and tradition are rich. If this psychoanalytical wisdom goes only half-way, is this not because it does not take adequately into account the deep reality which is in every human heart, the third dimension which it quickens and heals? This is how Fred Blum describes the possibilities of a therapy which resolutely takes into account this spiritual source in each being:

> When two people meet in their essence, at the core of their being, they are touching a truly shared deeper reality of life. They enter a relationship nourished by the Source of Life. They can see each other truly and their perception is illumined by a transpersonal light. We may 'fall in love' with another person and find out later that we do not really love the person as he or she actually and essentially is. The 'loved' person may have aroused certain projections in us which vanished as time went on. But if we truly love another person, a deeper reality sanctifying our love comes alive.
>
> In an actual human relationship both poles are likely to be activated: a deeper reality is coming to life but we also project something on the other person. This is also true in the relationship of the therapist and the person seeking to be healed. In the psycho-analytical literature the problem of projections has hitherto been prominent.

> There is no doubt that the greatest possible
> consciousness of this mechanism is essen-
> tial in order to avoid interference with the
> healing process. But the healing power
> alive in this process is not mediated through
> what has been called 'the transference/
> counter-transference' relationship which is
> essentially a projective mechanism, rather
> it comes alive through a quality of related-
> ness in which a shared deeper reality of life
> which unites us at our center, in our es-
> sence, is activated. A pre-condition for this
> to happen is that the therapist must have a
> living relationship to this reality.[1]

This very personal intimate reality which lies in the heart of each of the partners and is at the same time transpersonal, including both actors in a communion which surpasses them, irresistibly reminds the believer of a saying of Jesus: 'Where two or three are gathered in my name, there I am in the midst of them' (Mt 18:2). In the end, one realizes that it is the mysterious presence of Jesus at the heart of every human relationship which consti-tutes the only true dynamism of healing. He it is who is able to overcome the pitfalls of transfer, however subtle they may be, and enable us to benefit as much as possible from the transfer, because the Lord is always 'greater than the heart' (1 Jn 3:20) of man. What would here be undue extrapolation for the psychoanalyst careful not to go be-yond the limits of his field, the believer can have a premo-nition of and, under certain conditions, discern in the marvels which accompaniment allows him to witness from time to time.

---

1. Fred Blum, *Depth Psychology and the Healing Ministry* (London, 1990) 71.

The Dialogue of Accompaniment 5

WE HAVE SEEN HOW THE QUALITY of spiritual accompaniment depends in the first place on the quality of the human relationship which underlies it. The quality of a human relationship is reflected partly in the quality of the dialogue established between the two partners. Tradition is unanimous on this point: accompaniment is founded on a dialogue. In the egyptian desert, monks visited each other to ask the perennial question: 'How can I be saved? Father, give me a word.'

According to the witness of this same Tradition, this dialogue had a very precise object: the monks, according to the sources, asked the Fathers about their *logismoi,* a greek word which we usually translate as 'thoughts'. From this comes the universal practice in ancient monasticism which we call 'opening of the heart', also called 'manifestation of thoughts'. Saint Benedict kept a trace of this in his Rule in the fifth degree of humility, where he mentions it as something that goes without saying and posed no problem. Very likely the *confessio* referred to in twelfth-century monastic texts—particularly Saint Bernard's—has nothing to do with the sacrament of reconciliation as we know it today. It was probably instead an allusion to this same practice, which little by little died out during the following centuries, at least in western monasticism. In the East, it is still in favor in the great monastic centers like Mount Athos, Romanian Orthodox monasteries, and the coptic monasteries of Egypt.

In what does this manifestation of thoughts nowadays consist for our eastern brothers? On Mount Athos, for example, in a monastery which we might call of the strict observance, this is how it is usually practiced. Once a day, usually after the Office which ends the day, the monk goes to his spiritual father to give him an account of his 'thoughts'. This is not sacramental confession, but a quick sharing of all the good or less than good desires which manifested themselves in the course of the day. To render *logismos* as 'desire' seems an excellent translation, connected to the ancient etymology of the word and especially the contemporary practice of the manifestation of thoughts. To be sure, it can mean temptations or sins really committed, but this is certainly not the main object of such a manifestation. It is rather the desires, sometimes in the form of concrete projects which rise up in his heart all day long; these the brother simply comes to share with his elder. He expects from him neither absolution nor forgiveness, but something more fundamental, and no doubt also much more important: at the end of the sharing, the spiritual father contents himself with 'blessing' his son and then dismissing him. Most of the time, this is done without other words.

This sharing generally takes only a few—scarcely two or three—minutes. Other brothers are waiting in line, moreover. (This sometimes takes place in church before the iconostasis.) If the spiritual father had remarks or observations to make, they would be brief, but most often there are none. This is, moreover, not a real 'discernment' in the strict sense of the word. There is not enough time for that. Besides, the spiritual father and the brother in question know each other very well. It is enough to speak, to open oneself. It is the sharing which is important and which seems by itself to be effective, as well as the blessing which follows, which confirms what is good and heals what may be less good. A rite like this, for someone able to witness discreetly from a distance, distills a climate of great sweetness and at the same time strength. No impression of inhibiting culpability results, but, on the contrary, a sense of freedom and joyous spontaneity finally regained. A climate suitable for sharing is evidently very important, but this practice is fruitful only if certain conditions are respected.

To say this much is already partially to answer a question which might have occurred to the reader: is such a practice transposable as it is into a western setting? The time has not yet come to answer this question. First we must look closely at the very structure of this practice. By the end of this undertaking, the reader will have found the answer. Whatever it is, we may foresee that it will be black and white. In our religious culture today, when a rite such as this, practiced in so systematic a way, has become totally foreign to our usages, it would surely not be appropriate to reintroduce it precipitously. Under no circumstances should it be made compulsory. That goes without saying. For such a practice to have some chance of bearing fruit, the brother or sister must first freely have desired it. One may always speak about it, explain how it used to be done and is still today in the East. Even to propose that they try it would not be appropriate. It is preferable to wait until this desire arises in their hearts, inspired by the Holy Spirit, in great peace and with great freedom. Then only could an attempt be made, prudently, adapted to the psychological makeup of each. It is really not as simple as it first appears to someone who generously wishes to engage in it. In most cases, the brother or sister lets him or herself in for a trial which may be difficult, but which might also bear extraordinary fruits of liberation and peace.

It is, moreoever, evident that our dialogues of accompaniment today do not always occur at such a depth, even when they occur between a novice master and novice. Yet, although our partners do not engage in so systematic a manifestation of their desires, it often happens that they come to see us to confide something which touches their desires closely or somewhat remotely: a worry, a tension, a temptation, perhaps something they believe to be a sin.

These are confidences which are never easy to make and which they would not make to just anyone. In the beginning, we must expect them to come and confide any old thing, good or evil, because few are able right away to sort out the realities of life in the Spirit. They have borrowed their sense of values from a sort of prevailing morality, universally recognized by the culture of their day, a morality which is surely respectable, but whose dynamism does not necessarily conform in every respect to the Gospel's, even when this prevailing morality prescribes, forbids, raises guilt-feelings, or condemns. Even so, up to a certain point, the western accompanist finds himself confronted with a situation which is not unanalogous to that of the spiritual father in the Orthodox tradition.

At the beginning of the dialogue, the climate is sovereignly important: above all it must be one of listening and non-judgment. 'Non-judgment' here means the absence of all judgment in one sense or another. The brother who comes to confide asks neither for absolution nor condemnation. In the strict sense of the word, he does not come for encouragement. At the very beginning, when the brother comes to confide his deepest desires, pardon, condemnation and even encouragement would not be appropriate. Reactions of this sort would therefore be misplaced, because, even with the best intention in the world, they could impede sharing or even make it ineffective. The reader will have further opportunity to learn why at greater length. Here we need only remember what the deepest desire of the brother is who comes thus to confide his 'thoughts'. It is extremely important that, before any condemnation and before any encouragement, this brother be allowed to exist before someone else just as he reveals himself, as he is and as he experiences himself, even overwhelmed with shame, even eaten away by remorse. The first relief to offer him is permission to exist just as he is, the chance to exist before us just as he experiences himself, even if it is obvious to us that he experiences himself

in an incorrect or too disadvantageous a way. Is he con-
temptible and hateful in his own eyes? What does that
matter? With him is someone who welcomes him *talis
qualis:* as he is, omitting nothing, without any reservation, without the slightest reticence. 'A friend', said
Antoine Saint-Exupéry, 'is above all one who does not
judge.' We could say the same of the spiritual father: 'The
father is above all one who does not judge', after the image of the Father in heaven who makes his sun rise on the
just and on sinners. In both cases, he is father, nothing
more—father of the prodigal son as much as of the elder
son who stayed home.

To have permission to exist in front of another person
in love, to be accepted by him as one is, without any dis-
gust, with all the desires teeming in one's heart: this is the
fundamental desire of the person who comes to confide.
It is for the person accompanying him to listen to him
and welcome him as he is, totally, without excluding from
this welcome any level of his being from the lowest to the
highest. To welcome without reservation does not imply
approval. It is perfectly possible to welcome someone
deeply while holding reservations about his behaviour.
'Hate the vices, love the brethren', reminded Saint Benedict
(Rule 64.11). This is it exactly. Besides, once again, at this
stage of the dialogue, there is no question of approving or
condemning, but only of welcoming, of giving permission to exist in love. In a certain sense, this step is more
important than the following ones, because this is this
one which will forge the bond that will allow the relationship to evolve and bear fruit. If we miss it, there will
be no next stage, or the next stages will simply repeat the
scenario, and so be without gain for both persons. We
would unfailingly fall back into moralizing speeches, guaranteed in almost all cases to be without effect.

This first stage is more demanding for the one accompanying than it may at first seem. One might think that it
is enough to keep a strict silence, to let the other talk as

much as he wishes, and to forbid oneself scrupulously to intervene in any way. This is only partially correct, because such a technique constitutes only the external form of a listening attitude. It is not enough to keep silent. It might happen that while listening attentively to the other and while observing strict silence, the accompanist at gut level may speak without being able to control his interior monologue, which most of the time is completely unconscious. It could happen, for example, that the desires which the other confides or the vehemence with which he expresses them touch him very deeply and trouble him. He feels ill at ease, even threatened; he is afraid with a completely uncontrollable fear. The other's wounds have reopened secret wounds in him, and he can only protect himself from them as best he can, and thus violently reject the sentiments and desires which the other expresses in his presence. Here is an extreme case which can serve as an example. It is a true story. A bishop, who was approached by one of his priests to confide his decision to leave the priesthood to marry, found no other answer to give him than to seize the ashtray on the table in front of him and throw it at the priest's head. The gesture is very eloquent. The secret this priest had confided so touched the bishop in his own uncertainties about celibacy that he felt dizzy and could react only by this panic-stricken gesture. Celibacy was justified and defended by brute force alone. This is obviously a way of doing things which is not always effective. It is surely not the Good News announced in the Gospel.

Of course, a sensible accompanist will not react as this bishop did, even if the other's confided secret has caused a real tumult in his heart of hearts. He is too well brought up for that, and too attached to his self-image as a good accompanist. So he will try to keep silence and try his best not to have his face betray the revulsion or the fear he experiences interiorly. This is already something. But this is not enough because, without knowing it and without the other being able clearly to express it, he will have a gut reaction to his accompanist's malaise, even though the other cannot do anything about it. Even if he says nothing and makes no gesture, the other will feel repelled, ostracized, judged. In fact, every conversation is an interaction between gut reaction and discursive interchange, with the former being more direct in its effects than discourse itself. This rich form of communication allows a level of sharing which—unfortunately—has been almost completely forgotten and denigrated in our western culture, while it is still fluently used and understood in other countries. This is not so for Far Eastern people, who are culturally accustomed to this double mode of communication, a way of saying 'Yes' with their lips and yet communicating another message by the non-rational means of deep affectivity. Any interlocutor other than a Westerner is not fooled and decodes without effort or surprise the meaning of the information transmitted. The Westerner, however, clings to the idea of double talk and translates his uneasiness in terms unflattering to the Oriental or African: liar or hypocrite. This is not the case. They are not speaking or listening on the same wavelength! Underdevelopment may perhaps not be where we think it is: Orientals and Africans master a level of communication that we are far from equaling.

This fact is of far-reaching consequence for the dialogue of accompaniment. Far more important than the words of welcome or non-judgment are the feelings—as sincere as possible—of welcome and non-judgment we experience. It is good to specify 'as sincere as possible', because it would be of no use to pretend, even with the best of intentions. We are here precisely in an area where we can force nothing, an area which escapes our direct grasp and where our capacity to experience depends principally on the contact we have been able to establish and feel with the source of life at the deepest part of ourselves. To the degree to which we are really able to welcome the other person at this level, with the full weight of what he believes to be his misery, this welcome will immediately have an extremely beneficial result. The rest is only a sham welcome and adds an additional complication to a capacity for relationship already undermined enough.

A recent school of psychology uses the word empathy to describe this attitude of unconditional welcome. It supposes a bit more than the attitude of benevolent neutrality counseled by other theoreticians of the therapeutic dialogue. It implies a welcome of the person in depth, more or less as it has just been described here. Precisely because the person has been welcomed in this way, a positive evolution can begin. Empathy is not active and does not intervene by itself, but it conceals a force which is able to liberate in the other person a dynamism which will move it towards healing. The best description of empathy is found in Saint Paul when he describes *agapé* in the first Letter to the Corinthians: 'Love is patient, kind, never jealous, does not seek its own interest, is not irritable, takes no account of evil, excuses everything, believes everything, hopes everything, endures everything' *(13:4-7)*. That only love can heal is a well-known fact.

As we said earlier, it is not enough to refrain from judging and condemning–'You should be ashamed; you should stop acting like that'–we must also refrain from reassuring, encouraging, or approving, at least at this first stage of the dialogue. This kind of reaction would be just as harmful as a condemnation and, in some ways, perhaps even more harmful. This may surprise readers. The profound reasons for this assertion will become clear later on, but we point it out now—not least because today we are less inclined to make people feel guilty than we are exposed to the temptation to excuse and reassure them. Many accompanists or confessors sometimes give the impression that they spend most of their time dispensing 'good words' like: 'Today—that is, after Vatican II—we no longer consider that a sin; besides, you would not have had the time to consent; you were surely not completely free, or even completely conscious', and so on. Such words may seem soothing and reassuring at first glance. They are, however, not truly liberating, because they still refer the listener to the categories of permitted and forbidden, leading him to believe that, despite everything, he has still kept all the rules and is consequently worthy of our love and esteem. Precisely by reassuring him in this way, we strengthen the unconscious pattern from which he has been suffering for so long, namely, the supposition that one must have kept all the rules to be worthy of esteem and love. Every word which can be taken in this sense is a complete waste of effort and can only reinforce his uneasiness and block.

Besides, the person doing the talking has not come to ask for a certificate of good behavior, even if he sometimes gives that impression. From the moment that the person accompanying him tries to give him one, he is no longer able really to help him. Once again, what the other person profoundly desires, what he unconsciously, but with all his strength, aspires to, is to be reconciled with himself, and more particularly with the darkest and most confused place in himself where he discerns only wounds, wrongs, and faults. The only way for him to open himself to this reconciliation is the relationship he is weaving with his accompanist. It is as if, unconsciously, he were saying: 'Oh, if you, at least, could welcome me just as I am, continue to love me despite everything I confide in you.'

Through this unspoken request, he is in fact addressing God in person. An accompanist's most important task is to welcome the other person as God welcomes him. God never says to us: 'I love you because you are beautiful', but 'I love you because you are you, however you are, and whatever your sins and wrongs'. The only attitude, beyond all words, which can solace the other person and reconcile him with the darkest parts of his personality, those of which he is ashamed or afraid, is unconditional welcome, synonymous with love. Such a love, when it is true, when it springs from the deepest part of our being, is amply sufficient. Any additional word would simply be in the way.

Discovering such even–handedness in his attitude to the other person's confided secret deeply commits the person who listens and can constitute a painful awakening to the flaws in the accompanist's own psychological makeup. This awakening can become very fruitful. Let us go back to the extreme example of the ecclesiastical superior throwing an ashtray at the head of the priest who comes to announce his departure from the clerical state. By counter-attacking with such violence, he betrayed his own anguish in the presence of the wound which has just been revealed in the other person. But be careful! The accompanist who, far from counter-attacking in this way, might seek only to reassure, would find himself in exactly the same situation. Only the tactic he adopts is different. By his need to reassure, he too proves that he is not at peace with his desires either. The good words he bestows on the other serve as much to comfort him as to reassure the one he intends to accompany. He too is not really able to listen and welcome what the other comes to confide. In both cases, the unconscious objective is the same: to stop at any cost the baring of the partner's wounds. Only the tactics differ: either throwing an ashtray at him, or hiding his deep wound and minimizing its gravity by drowning it in a wave of mitigating circumstances. The person accompanied will leave the dialogue either appalled in the first case, or temporarily comforted, but his basic problem has not been addressed. In both cases, the dialogue ends in failure.

Listening to and unconditionally welcoming the other in dialogue—empathy—can go infinitely further. Let us return for a moment to what was said in the previous chapter about the transferential situation in which the person accompanying and the one accompanied find themselves involved together. Whether we like it or not, the transfer is there. We know this already. Now, as it was described earlier, the person accompanied cannot help using this to repeat the scenario within the transfer. He will do this by assigning a very specific role to the one accompanying him: the role of father, mother, friend, lover, and so on. By doing this, he proves first that the listening has worked properly. He allowed him to speak in such a way that the scenario, usually hidden under all kinds of repressions and disguises, was able to surface. We have seen that this is an opportunity, but also that the role of accompanist becomes more difficult to manage.

In fact, his position seems paradoxical, because he both listens from a distance and is part of the scenario, both displays neutrality and is up to his neck in a role. He must at all costs keep his distance, to the point of becoming almost absent. In the role the person accompanied assigns to him within his scenario, there is, so to speak, strictly no one. But this absence must at the same time manifest a presence, since the accompanist's refusal to enter into the role in which the scenario wants to cast him signifies more deeply that there is in fact someone. Yet this someone is so consistent and real that he refuses to let himself be reduced to the role programmed in advance by the scenario. Why does he refuse? Simply because he loves. He loves not with the narcissistic love the person accompanied would like to receive to his advantage through the scenario and transfer, but with another love, the only true kind of love, which the person accompanied still does not know.

The role which the person accompanied assigns to his accompanist within his scenario can be positive or negative. The accompanist will become suddenly either supremely lovable or perfectly detestable, sometimes both in very rapid succession. He must both welcome the role and never give in to it. Under all circumstances, the listener must remain imperturbable. If he is the object of love, he must not take to himself the love offered. If he is the object of hatred, he must be without hatred and without disturbance himself, constant and imperturbable in his attitude, which must simply be a closeness with the one who, with him, is experiencing a very difficult crossing, a Passover mystery. Being imperturbable does not mean being indifferent. On the contrary, more necessary than ever is this very special love immanent to listening and to the role of accompanist, this love which constitutes its secret depth, without which listening would remain fruitless. Because the person being listened to nourishes himself on this love in order to cross to the other shore to which life, blocked in him until now, calls him.

As we can see, the listening and welcoming we have just described goes beyond listening pure and simple, listening which is supposedly neutral. It is never entirely neutral, as some would have it. But once again, this does not mean that the listener gives in to the role the other would like him to play within the transfer. He simply has to welcome and, once this is done, at the right time, evade it. He thus develops a very specific type of presence, which can break the inevitable spell of the scenario into which the person accompanied would like to drag him. He is completely present, but as 'other', totally consistent with his autonomous, free, and fully responsible being. As Maurice Bellet writes: 'It is certain that listening goes beyond listening as we commonly imagine it. Listening is being in the drama, perhaps an extreme drama which the person is living; to be there as if we were not there. Then listening is making another space'.[1]

So it is truly the meeting within the listening, but beyond listening—it might be better to say 'in the depths of the listening'—the encounter between some quality of being in the person accompanying and the scenario of the one accompanied which allows the latter to begin another

1. Maurice Bellet, *L'Écoute* (Paris: Desclée de Brouwer, 1989) 118.

history, if only he agrees to cross to the other shore. Let us listen once again to Maurice Bellet:

> In all this, listening goes beyond listening and the person listening finds himself involved in an adventure where what he is counts . . . It is this that acts, by his welcoming silence as well as by his listening word. He is thus not the master in all that we have just evoked. No doubt he is not even conscious of it. It happens . . . It is from this shore that he can signal—by his very listening—that it is possible to cross.[2]

LISTENING TO DESIRES

Now let us try to pinpoint in greater detail some effects of this listening—specifically in relation to spiritual accompaniment. Since the first and most customary element of it is opening the heart or manifestation of desires, let us look at what might be the consequences of this listening on the relatively complex world of our desires.

The realm of our desires or of the impulses which dwell within us is a particularly delicate thing to confront. Each person vaguely senses that the deepest and most important of these escape his conscious influence: what he knows of them is only the visible peak of an iceberg, the hidden portion of which is far more insidiously menacing than the part he thinks he can see and dares to affirm. Classical treatises on moral theology or ascetical and mystical theology of necessity approached the problem abstractly. Desires, temptations, and impulses were described and classified. The authors attempted to regulate them within categories of prescriptions and interdicts. Some-

---

2. Bellet, *L'Écoute*, p. 120.

times they were classified according to the degree of seriousness—which was sometimes called the degree of perversity. But they certainly avoided touching them directly.
As we said above, imaginary characters were even invented
and charged with the faults or sins under scrutiny. Rarely
did anyone deal with real cases; that would have been far
more complex and disturbing. In a word, they did not dirty
their hands. Until very recently, the most delicate parts of
such treatises on moral theology were written and taught
only in Latin, so threatening or completely indecent did
everyday words seem when describing certain things. Out
of prudence, the courses were even delayed until the very
outside limit of reasonable time: just before ordination. In
french seminaries, these courses were called *diaconales,*
because they were strictly reserved for deacons. Did this
delay result from an obscure need to protect them? Perhaps. No doubt people were also aware that a statement
of morality, even if necessary for various reasons, has no
real influence on the reality of desires. Its effectiveness is,
in fact, limited and even open to debate, to the degree that
such a statement risks producing negative effects as soon
as it is felt to be repressive, or to induce guilt, as unfortunately was often the case.

The world of desires is not a clear and simple world.
Our desires get tangled up in a complex and subtle way
which we must look at with some degree of humor. They
seem to join, to encourage, one another, to hide behind
other desires. One desire can mask another. We often get
the impression of never reaching the end of our desires,
like an onion, where layers hide more layers indefinitely.
What is more, we are vaguely conscious that we do not
know our most secret desires. Our culture has assimilated
the most basic facts of psychoanalysis well enough for us
to be rather irritated when any lapse, word, or failing
seems to betray in us desires which we would not admit
at any price, even to ourselves.

The reason is simple: not only are these desires difficult

to identify, but sometimes they are difficult to admit, because the world of our desires arouses in us a host of other feelings we barely keep under control. At the top of of this list come shame and guilt. If there is an area where guilt reigns supreme, this is it. The opening of the heart and even the sacrament of reconciliation seem painful to many people only because they feel themselves particularly exposed there to the tyranny of this shame, which weighs on them to the point of seriously deforming the meaning of their desires and actions. We touch here an area in which fault, sin, guilt, desires, temptations, and bad thoughts are particularly tangled. Since they constitute the special preserve of spiritual accompaniment, it is worth spending some time here.

In fact, discerning between good and evil is not always easy. Not objective evil—about that moral theology can say valuable things, as we have said—but subjective evil, evil for this concrete person, and the individual responsibility which it involves. In this realm, it is necessary to take a prudent step backward before judging. According to the title of an already old but still famous book, the *Virtues of the Vices and the Vices of the Virtues*[3] really exist. A person's true good is not infallibly that which presents itself as good, because a deformed desire bent back on itself can very well disguise itself as good and appear as such at a first, superficial glance. On this point, it is the same for good as for evil. Evil is even harder to unmask, in any case much more difficult than certain 'morality police' would lead us to believe. 'Evil can disguise itself as good' says the proverb, and Jesus reminded us that 'A wolf can disguise itself as a lamb' (Mt 7:15). But we must go further. We can say that here below, behind each appearance of evil, good is hiding. Let us be clear: we are talking about the appearance of evil, or a partial evil. Would

3. Paul Chauchard, *Vices des Vertus et Vertus des Vices* (Paris, 1963) ; cf. André Berge, *Les maladies de la vertu* (Paris 1960).

it be thinkable to encounter absolute evil among men or in a man? Evil in an absolute state does not exist here below. If it exists anywhere, it is in hell. Between persons, within a person, nothing is irretrievably evil. In every man, depraved as he may appear, there remains a good which it is always important to liberate and emphasize. It is the same with his desires. Underneath the strangest and sometimes the most fantastic desires and needs, a true need, a sometimes deep and absolutely vital desire is always hidden. This desire, more often than not, has not been emphasized and honored when it should have been. It was repressed, stifled. Now it is still waiting to be freed and perhaps even fulfilled.

Evil, they say, is often nothing more than a disguised good or desire. If there is evil, at least psychologically speaking, it is situated precisely in this disguise. It is never in the desire taken by itself, which is always fundamentally good. To speak of some desires as essentially good and other desires as essentially bad would be to borrow a manichean scheme of things and suppose that there exists in man a principle and forces which do not come from the sole Creator. But if transient evil consists here below in the disguise or distortion of desire, then it is important to free it from its disguise, to correct this distortion which spoils it. If such an operation were to succeed—and it never completely does—the remains of the desire would merge with the good. Now, the good which hides behind an apparently evil desire always deserves to be taken into consideration and honored for its true value. To say still more: the good which is in this desire deserves to be fulfilled, to the degree that it still can be.

There are no essentially evil desires, solely the result of diabolical action. If desires present themselves in sometimes strange forms, or urge someone to behavior which obviously has something in common with what we call sin, this is simply because they are not in the right place; because they are disordered, Saint Bernard would say. All desires can be ordered and put into place—we could also say structured—only by love. Only a true love orders desires. And if most people, not to say just about everyone, suffer from desires which they consider disordered, it is because we are all more or less wounded people, love-challenged.

Any desire can become dangerous only to the degree that it has not been ordered by a great love, or adequately fulfilled in the depths of the human person; but also to the degree that it does not, so to speak, join in, and has been able to take an independent and headlong course within the psyche; to the degree especially that it is a disguise for a deeper desire, a vital desire which has never yet been taken seriously and honored as it deserved. On the other hand, a desire which always springs from an absolute love, along with the suffering inherent to the frustration of its non-fulfillment, especially once this desire is correctly taken into account and fulfilled to whatever degree is still possible—the thousand small apparently evil desires which served as decoys lose their power to fascinate and are no longer experienced as an almost irresistible giddiness or as dangerous, quite contrary to how they seemed to be earlier.

How can the fundamental desire still be fulfilled to the degree to which it is still possible, as we have just suggested? It is here that the force of love—this 'strange love' Maurice Bellet[4] used to speak about, which shows itself in the accompaniment relationship—must play its role fully, a role we may term healing or therapeutic. If among human beings evil is very often only an unbalanced good, a good but disguised desire, this is because it is not yet adequately exposed to the heat of this sun which we call true love. Only the heat of true love is able little by little to straighten out the distortion of desire and allow the true good to manifest itself there. Indeed it is the need for love

4. Bellet, *L'Écoute*, p. 127.

which orders all the other desires, because all desires are reduced to their permanent source: the deepest desire in each person, the need to be fully and unconditionally welcomed in love. Only love in some fullness is able to structure all the other desires and put them in their true place.

It is the experience of such a love, too, and it alone, which will some day make possible a fertile and fruitful renunciation. Such a consequence is directly relevant to us, because the whole area of renouncing certain desires is part of the ground covered by spiritual discernment and accompaniment. A person who is led to renounce still badly ordered desires before the appropriate time, desires which are tangled up in each other and still serve as disguises or decoys for other, more vital and important desires, by making this sort of renunciation risks at the same time repressing the vital need hidden behind them. Besides, those desires appear fascinating or threatening only to the extent that something else much more important hides in them; often something else which no one can renounce, strictly speaking, without taking great risks. In the case of such a premature renunciation, the person is still not able truly and fully to renounce them. On the contrary, under cover of renunciation, he risks amputation. Without his knowledge, and a real generosity notwithstanding, he represses, to use the technical term, a fundamental part of his being. The result of such an operation, despite the good intentions and the fervor it demonstrates, obviously remains very unpredictable—not to say frankly doubtful. The vital desire thus repressed will continue to work in the unconscious and will not take long to reappear under other disguises, in more and more subtle or ridiculous forms. As long as the vital desire has not yet been able to detach itself from its accidental disguises, and someone's total efforts are directed to the disguises rather than to the act of listening, recognizing, and welcoming this vital desire, they will continue to exert pressure and even ravage by means of intervening disguises.

On the other hand, in the case of truly positive renunciation, the reverse happens. This presupposes that one has first let the desire rise to consciousness and has become aware of it, peacefully and objectively. Whatever it is, this desire is never evil, and it is good to be able to face it, quietly, without fear, but also without recklessness, recognize it as one's own, as part of oneself and eventually of one's development, if the person concerned chooses to fulfill it. In a certain sense, one needs first to be fully reconciled with this desire. In most cases, this can occur only under the gaze of another, a gaze of love, by a person who unconditionally welcomes, empowers, makes allowances, confirms. Looking at this desire together with a gaze of love permits them to flush out all that the person was still hiding unawares, all his distortions and curves. The love which this person experiences in this way is able little by little to straighten the contortions of desire, rip away disguise, liberate a far more fundamental need for love, one which no disguise can exhaust or exalt, and which is called to be fulfilled some day beyond anything one could consciously desire for the present; a need for love which, as far as possible, deserves to be fulfilled right away. As a result, the superficial desire loses its fascination, compulsion, irresistibility, because the giddiness of desire is strong only to the degree to which it is identified with a more vital desire which is, strictly speaking, irrepressible. As soon as this is sufficiently liberated and fulfilled, it becomes possible and even relatively easy to renounce the superficial desire peacefully and without harm. From then on, one is able to renounce without mutilating or destroying oneself. Because one renounces in this way out of love, or out of a beginning of love, one can do it in joy and at the same time grow in humanness. It is always love and joy which command renunciation. The form of love which a person renounces really tempts him—why not?—but he still can renounce it in perfect freedom in favor of a love experienced as more urgent, because the first kind no longer fascinates him as much. It has lost its compulsive character because the vital desire which was hiding behind it is fulfilled elsewhere and with infinitely more gratification.

Dr Fred Blum, already quoted above, makes this comment on the words of Jesus in *Mt 16:24-26,* on the need for the disciple of Jesus to love his life in order to find it:

> Jesus said to his disciples: 'If anyone wishes to be a follower of mine, he must leave self behind: he must take up his cross and come with me. Whoever cares for his own safety is lost: but if a man will let himself be lost for my sake, he will find his true self. What will a man gain by winning the whole world at the cost of his true self? Or what can he give that will buy back that self?'
>
> These words are paradoxical: to lose in order to find, to receive by giving. For such an admonition to be meaningful, we must first have gained what we are asked to lose. We cannot lose something that we do not possess. We must first develop a strong 'I' and be on our way to true self-realization before we can take up our cross and follow him. Until these conditions have been fulfilled, we . . . cannot find anything by losing. We must have reached the stage of development where we can move into the realm of the paradox before we can find our true self by losing all those tendencies and qualities which are ego-centered rather than true-self centered.
>
> The way in which the call to lose ourselves was understood in the Victorian era and still often is today, was tragic because it led to stunted rather than to fulfilled

lives, the opposite of what it was intended to be. The roots of this tragedy lie in a conception of 'egoism' and 'altruism' which failed to distinguish between the true self and the little self and which kept the understanding of selfhood within the realm of the opposites. As a result it considered a concern with one's own development in opposition to a concern for others. It was an either-or attitude rather than a giving-and-receiving experience—a paradox which was already expressed in the Biblical injunction: 'Love your neighbour as yourself' *(Mt 22: 38)*. We must love ourselves by truly responding to the call to develop our God-given potentialities in order to become the kind of person whom we are meant to be. This is the foundation for a self-giving love through which we receive more than we give rather than losing by giving. Giving from the overflow of our heart enriches us while it enriches others. Love thus understood is the hallmark of our true humanity—the ultimate test of health.[5]

The only criteria for a fruitful renunciation are love and joy. And above all joy, because it springs from love and can never again be separated from it. This is also Saint Benedict's last criterion in permitting a monk to add something to his usual *ascesis* in Lent: that he be able to do it 'in the joy of the Holy Spirit', *cum gaudio Sancti Spiritus offerat Deo* (Rule, 49). Only our deepest joy allows a true discernment of our desires. It alone can authenticate renunciation.

5. Blum, *Depth Psychology and the Healing Ministry* (London 1990) 27-28.

TWO INNER AUTHORITIES: The POLICEMAN 6

OW WE ARE GOING TO GO deeper into
the concrete strategy, so to speak, of spiritual accompaniment. After becoming aware of transference, its risks and opportunities, we looked at the qualities of welcome and listening which must be present at
any opening of the heart: attentive listening, so concen-
trated, so charged with presence and love that it becomes
active and effective. At this point in our analysis, two com-
ponents of spiritual accompaniment will be described in
detail. These two elements intervene as much in the person accompanying as in the one being accompanied. They
are intrinsically part of the scenario of each, and so they
inevitably interfere with the transference within which
the dialogue of accompaniment takes place. They exercise
a certain authority, a strange, almost always unconscious,
power over the psyche of both persons. This particularity
makes of them real authorities. In other words, and to put
it into an image, these two elements or authorities present
themselves to us as an inner policeman and an interior
mirror. As it will appear further on, these two authorities
are very similar, they lead into one another but are not
entirely identical, because their respective roles in the evolution of a concrete psychology are generally very distinct.

Like the transference or the scenario, these two authorities are not anomalies which can appropriately be got rid
of. On the contrary, they are normal structures inherent
to every healthy psyche; without them no one could live
or breathe psychically. Only their potential weight, or the
abusive role they can play, can—in some cases—become
so inordinate that they disturb the normal evolution of
the person. More than a disturbance, in certain extreme

but not exceptional cases, this can be a matter of a psychic paralysis which can retard or seriously compromise spiritual growth without a miracle of grace, which is always a possibility. It is indispensable not only to be aware of their existence, but also to have a certain concrete experience of them in oneself and in others. Nothing is as valuable as being able to catch our own or our interlocutor's inner policeman or mirror in the act.

This is even more true—and on this we must insist—in light of transference and the scenario, because these two authorities constantly crop up in spiritual dialogue and in listening, even if we would like them to be objective and detached. We must not hide this fact from ourselves. By claiming to welcome the confidences of another person, we are penetrating—breaking and entering, as it were—into an area usually reserved for these two authorities, their private place, in the strict sense, in which they expect to exercise a quiet domination, not to say a real tyranny. These two authorities know perfectly well what are the desires, temptations, good or evil actions, honesty or dishonesty, virtues or vices, and they can only react more or less violently, more or less subtly, but most of the time very effectively against the undue intrusion of a third party which would like to be welcoming and, they claim, 'neutral' in an area they have long since classified and judged.

These two authorities can play an analogous role in relation to God or rather the image of God that each person has constructed, which is often only an idol which these two authorities have actively collaborated in developing more or less successfully. These are our false gods. We must realize that they are very real to us and it is not easy to evict them. They are idols fashioned by our unconscious 'in the image and likeness' of what we are, that is, of man. All this takes shape by a phenomenon of projection which is an antithetical parody of God's creation of man. Since these two authorities are very attached to their role, or rather, since *we* are very attached to them without knowing it, one of the basic problems in any listening will be identifying and neutralizing them as much as possible. The true God is beyond or before these idols, never in the place they abusively hold.

THE INNER POLICEMAN

The first authority we meet has been called, not unhumorously, the 'inner policeman'. He is in connivance with our idols because he also is posted and swings into action at the very place where we are called to be attentive to the one we have called the 'inner Master'. Who or what is it? In the unconscious of each one of us, there takes place, from earliest childhood on, a sort of crystallization of the traces and echoes left behind by every person who has exercised authority over us. Psychology calls this the 'super-ego', an inner authority which plays an important role, not only in the life of every human being, but also in the progressive development of a common culture and the morality which flows from it.

This crystallization is the result of a complex process, because all sorts of echoes are clustered there: the echo of must-do's and don't-do's imposed on us; the echo of punishments we have received; the echo of faults we have been accused of. It is obvious that this interior authority has a special link with each person's unconscious memories of his father, especially if he has played the role a father usually plays in his child's life—that is, the person who imposed the first important taboos which constitute the child's personality. This is not only a normal, but an eminently desirable, phenomenon. By doing this, the father reveals himself fully as father, and the taboo, if it is accepted and assimilated in love, will mark the son's psychological makeup forever.

Traces of the father's authority are not the only determining influences. Other authorities have succeeded it and continued to mold the unique identity of the interior policeman. First of all, there is the mother's role which, up to a point, can make up for a more or less absent father. In addition, there is everyone who has been an authority during the life of the child and adolescent: teachers, those in charge of youth groups, priests and spiritual directors, novice masters, religious superiors, and so on. From then on, everything in life having to do with virtue or vice, exterior good manners or propriety, is in practice under the unconscious control of this inner policeman. He is the one who still forbids certain things, evaluates others—this is good, this is evil. Sometimes he prevents us from acting, he makes us fail, or he threatens us, he feeds our fear. He even goes so far as to punish us or slap us in the face. He is especially good at arousing and keeping alive strong feelings of shame and guilt.

Before being active in each of us, the inner policeman is also active in the prevailing culture and its morality . Before being under the control of our own inner policeman, moreover, each of us has already been formed, in a manner of speaking, by the policeman diffusely present in the culture within which we have grown up. Each culture has its own model of perfection which still remains essentially pagan, whatever the evangelical varnish covering it, even though it has always been somewhat influenced, at least in the West, by a long christian tradition. Nowadays, these models are extremely fluid and change far more quickly than in the past. The fact remains, however, that our unconscious will always be marked by the model of perfection which was dominant during our childhood. On the other hand, our unconscious will evolve in close dependence on the models presented by our parents and teachers. Becoming aware of the models of perfection specific to our time and to which we necessarily make sacrifices, to catch sight of their traces in our own ideals, feelings, or spontaneous reactions, can be an important element conducive to any spiritual discernment, because it is obvious that despite appearances, there will always be a perceptible gap between these models of perfection which are tied to a specific culture and holiness according to the Gospel. Whether we like it or not, our heart conceals some tiny idols before which we continue to burn our incense, and these spiritual accompaniment should progressively help us unmask.

Our psychology seizes on this model of perfection, inherited from the surrounding culture, adapts it and refines it to its use, forming in this way its own one-of-a-kind and original interior policeman, entirely at our service! With a little experience, it is relatively easy to recognize its presence and discern its interventions in the words and behavior of the person facing us in dialogue. The relationship which someone has with his own policeman betrays itself continuously in many ways. Let us think back to the scenario or transfer which, as Lacan says, is the 'revelation of the unconscious'. In the same way, the relationship with the interior policeman reveals itself in the way a person approaches the person accompanying him, says hello or ignores him, shakes his hand or remains at a distance, speaks or remains silent, sits on his chair or remains standing; in a word, in the way he locates himself concretely in his relationship with the accompanist.

The policeman betrays himself especially in the vocabulary used. Several stereotyped formulas in current use often introduce a direct manifestation of the policeman and his demands: 'I should have . . .', 'I'm not allowed to . . .', 'It is unthinkable that . . .', 'I should be ashamed of . . .', 'I failed all my responsibilities by . . .', 'Please forgive me for . . .', 'I'm afraid of . . .', 'I'm afraid that . . .', and on it goes. We could add to the list. None of these formulas is neutral. They are always involved in the transfer inherent in every human relationship; an objective excuse for any exteriorization of the interior policeman. The privileged place which spiritual accompaniment gives favors these incursions of the policeman into everyday speech, and offers him, as it were, a mirror in which he becomes concrete. The experience of finding oneself in front of one's accompanist can only awaken in the person accompanied all the feelings related to the profile of his inner policeman. And as soon as he opens his mouth, he cannot avoid expressing them, either to defend himself from them and thus reject them, or on the contrary to embrace them as docilely as possible.

We could illustrate this by another example. The relationship to the inner policeman betrays itself in a particularly obvious way in a driver's spontaneous reaction when a real policeman (exterior this time!) signals him to stop along the road. These reactions can vary a great deal. For example, a wave of guilt: 'What could I have done?' or an uncontrollable need to win the policeman's sympathy: 'Yes, officer', 'Of course, officer, 'I agree completely, officer', 'At your service, officer'. The opposite reaction can prevail: a violent rejection which escapes in a swearword and goes so far as an attempt to flee or break through a police roadblock. These reactions are normal. They can be explained in part by the action of an unconscious psychological confrontation between the inner policeman and the authority facing him, which can go all the way to assimilation pure and simple. In this last case, how authority has worked in the life of that individual and the feelings that go along with it dictate the impulsive reactions. This example, taken from daily life, is basically no different from the crystallization of reactions in play during spiritual accompaniment. An inevitable identification is at work: the person accompanying little by little takes on the inner policeman's features.

This identification is helped, but at the same time, somewhat complicated by the fact that within the relationship an inner policeman is activated not only in the person accompanied but also in the person accompanying. Obviously, it is important that the latter be aware of this and be somewhat familiar with the features of his own inner policeman. On both sides, in fact, the two policemen cannot avoid entering into dialogue and often into conflict, a perfectly unconscious dialogue and conflict, of course, but one which could have negative effects without some discernment. This presupposes on the part of the accompanist a distance from his own policeman, his being in a position to foil its interventions or at least to manage them with full knowledge of the situation because he is aware of them. This presupposes in him an experience of contact with his deep being and the understanding, at least by hearsay, of what it means 'to be led by the Holy Spirit'.

To the extent this last condition is insufficiently fulfilled, the person accompanying will inevitably listen to all that is confided to him with the ears of his own inner policeman and to risk being irresistibly led to take over that role: he will judge, threaten, scare, arouse feelings of shame and guilt: 'You should be ashamed', even if he tries to keep silent and succeeds in not expressing his feelings aloud, as we have already seen. But the somersaults or convulsions of his own inner policeman will be more than enough to spoil the climate of unconditional welcome which should govern the exchange. The person accompanying may not notice, but the one accompanied will feel uneasy to the degree that he obscurely feels his own inner policeman being struck full-force by the reactions of his counterpart in the accompanist. He will indeed be ashamed, feel guilty, and try to expiate and find favor with him again.

In this way, the opportunity this exchange offers for a hoped-for interior event is seriously compromised. And all because the person accompanying is still the victim of his own policeman and tries to take over the role of policeman to the person coming to confide in him. The result is simple but unfortunate: the interior Master, the Holy Spirit, will not be able to arise at the heart of the relationship, to exercise his clarifying and salvific action on the desires put into words. A dialogue will in fact have taken place, but at a totally different level; a dialogue which can only reinforce all the negative feelings surrounding the admission. Because the love-filled silence which welcomes the admission of desire was there specifically to allow a deeper level of the person to surface, the level of true love which orders and fulfills all desires.

In every case, the accompanist finds himself carried away in a confrontation which occurs both within the person accompanied and within the relationship. Whether he likes it or not, the person is thereafter part of this confrontation, and its outcome will depend in great measure on his attitude. Nor will he himself come out of it unscathed.

In what does this confrontation consist? It is simple. In traditional terms, we would say it consists in correcting a false conscience and replacing it by a right conscience. In psychological terms closer to the spiritual reality, we would say that it consists in neutralizing the harmful influence of the interior policeman or the super-ego and allowing the Holy Spirit to take it over by love. Now, the inner policeman always risks suffocating deep life within man, whereas the Holy Spirit and his Law of love are the only source of true life.

For the confrontation to be positive, the first condition is obviously that the person accompanying not move into someone else, as it were, replacing his inner policeman, and thus leading to a regrettable identification with this policeman. This pitfall is not always avoided by the accompanist—far from it—and it dooms his intervention to failure in advance. This substitution neutralizes all the hoped-for liberating effects; what is worse, it accentuates the paralyzing action of the inner policeman: without knowing it, the accompanist has given him the upper hand. It has then become pointless meddling at a level different from deep life, which is prevented from welling up.

Here we have entered a vicious circle, difficult to break. The accompanist is added to the 'syndrome', if we may call it that. From now on he is part of it. Of course, he can always expend himself in speaking and giving advice and information. He can forbid, permit, encourage, call on a sense of responsibility—all of which generally does no harm, but in this instance, no longer does any good. His words act only in the sphere of influence of the inner policeman with whom he is in league from now on, whereas his first objective should have been to neutralize that influence so that another influence could make itself felt, one springing up from a depth with which any possibility of contact is now temporarily cut off.

We must also point out that the person accompanied, without knowing it, collaborates in the elaboration of this psychological pitfall in step with the accompanist. He will do all he can to connect with him and make him his inner policeman's accomplice. This is the most comfortable situation for him. Despite his explicit request, he is not yet really disposed to grow. He experiences a spontaneous giddiness, sometimes real anguish at anything which might require him to go beyond the scenario, this habit by which he thereafter gets along with his inner world and with others. If anyone takes it upon himself to echo his inner policeman and repeat that he is forbidden to do certain things under pain of a guilt deserving punishment, then he is again confirmed in his accustomed reactions, measuring himself only by what is the least disturbing or threatening for him at the time. In fact, behind a punishment virtuously requested or accepted emerges the hope of once again having fulfilled all the rules and thus implicitly being worthy of esteem and love.

Generally and unambiguously, the trap the person accompanied lays for his guide this way reveals itself in the resistance which he will soon put up against his accompanist, who for his part is working hard to escape this identification's grasp. If the latter delays in echoing his inner policeman's reproaches and warnings, he will experience increasing irritation and uneasiness which he will certainly manifest by words and actions. He will, for instance, say that he is misunderstood and frustrated by his guide. He may also resort to a few subtle manoeuvers of blackmail or retaliation. If, despite all this, the accompanist does not yield, he will in the end abandon him for good to seek elsewhere, in a less aware guide perhaps, a policeman more indulgent to his own.

Inversely, if the accompanist has bought into the words of the other person's inner policeman, the latter's calm will generally not last very long, because such an attitude on the accompanist's part can only strengthen the policeman's harmful words. Thus validated, he will reappear without delay, inspiring an ever more inaccessible ideal of virtue, dragging the subject into the indefinite spiral of the ego's demand for perfectibility, increasing the distance between it and the deep self and making up an ideal ever more divergent from the reality of his deepest desires.

The process which should have taken place at the heart of the relationship of accompaniment has simply been short-circuited. It is aborted before really having started, when it should have dealt with breaking the policeman's spell. The accompaniment was supposed to be the counterweight by which it would have been possible to escape his grasp, by dodging and somehow passing behind him rather than confronting him, and being able to descend more deeply within oneself, there to be confronted with the swarm of one's desires—which is complex, as we have already seen, but which only appears threatening. It is vital that each person—psychologically, but also spiritually, speaking—be able to recognize his desires along with their share of distortion and also with all their truth and vitality. To look at them and approve them as truly ours would allow us to present them just as they are to the beneficial activity of our deep self and of grace, because it is there, both at the deepest part of our heart teeming with all these desires and at our most extreme weakness, that grace awaits us.

The inner policeman's whole strategy seems to consist precisely in sparing us this moment of truth and obscuring our weakness by making us believe that under certain conditions—that is to say, by respecting a slightly burdensome collection of taboos that he himself has made for anyone who cares to listen to him—it is possible to play by all the rules and play the virtuous man or the virtuous Christian, satisfied and satisfactory, reassured and reassuring. When this strategy succeeds, its consequences are negative. It becomes impossible for someone to bring his desires to light in order to be able to accept them peacefully. On the contrary, all one's effort consists in repressing them and defending oneself from them. The spiritual consequences are even more serious. If it is possible to play by all the rules perfectly this way, then grace is of no avail. Such a person would be one of those of whom Jesus said in the Gospel, 'they are convinced that they are just and do not need mercy' *(Lk 18:9)*. The Pharisees in the Gospel represent this kind of 'just man', both psychologically and spiritually. They were certainly fulfilling all the rules, and by this very fact were excluded from Jesus' message and interest, he who had come, as he loved to underline, 'not for the just, but for sinners' *(Mt 9:13 ; Mk 2:17 ; Lk 5:32)*.

Maybe we are more sensitive nowadays to the extreme importance of the first words spoken by the accompanist after a secret has been confided. They can have incalculable consequences. They will set the relationship on a certain course and will decide its consequences, positive or negative. It is important to weigh them carefully and to speak only advisedly, avoiding anything that might permit collusion between the accompanist and the inner policeman of the one accompanied. We may think that generally–*salvo meliori iudicio*–the accompanist is too quick to speak. Since any word is particularly risky here, it is almost always preferable to leave a long silence before speaking.

To sum up briefly what we have said: neither guilt-inducing comments ('You should be ashamed!'), nor good words of encouragement aimed to exonerate the subject are appropriate, because only the level of permitted-forbidden is conjured up, skewing the face to face encounter which alone is liberating. The scenario remains structurally the same: the policeman now permits what had been forbidden. This permutation is still set within a moralizing framework, not in the movement of deep life, where our desires are waiting to be confronted with the light and warmth of the Holy Spirit.

We must admit that, in practice, it is often hard not to enter into collusion with the other person's inner policeman. In this regard, we should be attentive to this kind of comment from him: 'I should have done this or that'; 'From now on I will have to watch out for . . .'. They are to be neither approved nor refuted. We need only listen to them. The fact that they provoke no reaction, either positive or negative, from the accompanist is already in itself extremely important. Since they do not arouse any echo where echo was expected, phrases like this—which are important for the person accompanied—get lost in the void. They have no impact on anything or anyone. The emotional force behind them will disintegrate that much faster, almost by itself, without the least intervention of the one accompanying. By persevering untiringly in non-intervention and by offering no foothold to his partner's inner policeman, the accompanist multiplies his subject's opportunities to listen to his deep self and desires. And is the desire that God has for him not the deepest desire in every human person, that is to say, the Holy Spirit, who, the Christian believes, is actively present in every human being?

Yet the systematic silence of listening can sometimes become painful to maintain. In some cases, instead of facilitating confidences from the person accompanied, it seems to paralyze them. How should we behave then? Several attitudes are possible. Sometimes it may be best simply to sit in deadlock, that is, to continue for a while in this silence, on the condition of taking time later to analyze together what is expressed in the uneasiness it causes. In fact, during such silence, the attitudes, gestures, looks, gut feelings speak infinitely more than could words.

Often it will be more useful—especially at the beginning of the relationship, in order to allow the other person to continue expressing himself—to interrupt the silence with phrases which try to reformulate in other words what he thinks he understood of the secret he has just confided. 'If I have understood you correctly, you mean that . . . Is that right? Do you recognize yourself in my words?'–'Yes, you have understood me'–'Then, let's go on.' An intervention like this is perfectly neutral, because it is at the level of the objectivity of the message sent: has this been correctly understood? If yes, the fact of having been understood often allows the speaker to step over the deadlock and progress in the dialogue. In case he felt that he was not understood, he could take this opportunity to repeat his confidence or add details important to him.

When the bond between accompanist and accompanied has established itself sufficiently in reciprocal confidence, this tactic of questioning can also be used to draw attention indirectly to certain unusual but significant elements in the speech of the person offering confidences: apparent yet transparent incoherence, oversights, lapses, tone, delivery, emotional vehemence of the expressions or images used. In all these cases, the important thing is to start from the very words used without judging them or interpreting them at an inopportune time, but asking him to comment on them himself. There is nothing more reassuring for him than his own words, which more than anything else give him the impression of being perfectly heard and understood.

Does this mean that the accompanist is to remain forever mute, as if he were forbidden to speak, and that he is condemned to persevere indefinitely in this strategy of non-intervention? Didn't the disciples of the first monks in the desert go to ask their Father specifically in order to receive a Word? 'Give me a Word, abba, to be saved!' The objection is entirely pertinent. In fact, the fundamental difference between a psychological journey—marked by empathy alone—and spiritual accompaniment, lies precisely in the fact that at the right time—and only at the right moment—the accompanist will not hesitate to pronounce a Word, in the strongest sense, whose psychological and therapeutic impact may be incalculable.

Why 'only at the right moment'? First, because it is important that the ground be sufficiently cleared. This is the role of respectful listening which refuses to become the ally of the speaker's inner policeman, so as to be able to see more clearly the—at first apparently inextricable—knot of desires and disguised desires we have just spoken of. This condition, as we have seen, is indispensable if deep life is to have some chance to manifest itself. Then, because, in a certain number of cases—more frequently that we usually think—attentive and affectionate listening is enough. It can, in fact, free a Word and response in the other which he alone possesses. In a certain sense, the accompanist does not possess a Word about the other person. It is first within the other, and the Word which the guide may pronounce about him can only awaken in him, as an echo, the Word which was already sleeping within him and which is an absolute prerequisite for any Word which might come to him from without.

And yet, one day a Word will have to be spoken. Is this not what characterizes all christian experience, where fraternal mediation appears as the normal condition? Such a Word can take on several forms and is not necessarily limited to the oral message. A look, a highly symbolic gesture, even a pause in speaking can have the same weight. If words are used, we may believe that they will be brief and very restrained. Because this has to do with a Word in the strong sense of the word: a foundational—one might almost dare say, creative—Word, as the Words of God are always creative, or, in its own way, like the word of a father, recognizing his son and calling him by name. This is one of the most amazing experiences we can have here below. This is why they are rare, surely unique to each of us.

This Word will spring up from the deepest part of the accompanist, to touch the other in his deep self. It will indeed 'spring up'. This will happen spontaneously, almost unexpectedly, sometimes even without the speaker's knowledge. It is useless to think ahead about such a Word or program it. Above all, it is impossible to pretend. The Word will be given at the right time, thanks to the very quality of the relationship, which gives the word its true effectiveness, because only love begets and gives life. This is the law of life which propagates itself. It goes without saying that the accompanist will be better able to speak such a Word if he himself has received one from another person who had taken the time necessary to listen to him, of his nagging doubts, to speak the Word which in the depths strengthened him once and for all, which identified him with some extraordinary force present in him from the beginning, but in which, left to himself, he would never have dared believe. Because this Word flowed from the source in his accompanist, that is, from his deep self, it touched him also in his deep self. What was evident in the former became, as it were, naturally evident for him as well. It was very simple. It was unique. Any other word would have been superfluous.

THE COUNTER-TRIAL: THE SCRUPULOUS PERSON

To give a concrete example of what we have just described, let us take the scrupulous person. This kind of case is, unfortunately, relatively frequent, but also especially transparent and among the most elementary. In fact, in such a person the inner policeman reveals itself in all its brutality and perversity. Yet the simplicity of this case is offset by its being also among the most difficult to manage in practice. Every spiritual director knows this frustrating side of the scrupulous person's fantasies. He is the typical example of someone completely, feet and wrists bound, handed over to the inner policeman's tyranny. This interior authority is so overdeveloped that practically all activity is forbidden and he is completely paralyzed. He always hears words like: 'You shouldn't do this, you shouldn't do that, it's a sin; besides you are already guilty, you can only make mistakes!' The scrupulous person presents himself as a walking super-ego, a inner policeman incarnate, for other people as much as for himself. The policeman rules as sovereign in his unconscious, even as a dictator and a real torturer. Not only in the subject's unconscious, for it overflows its field of consciousness and even tries to take over its neighbors' unconscious.

Those who have some experience of this know that it is not very pleasant to grapple with a scrupulous person who is forever bringing someone round to his viewpoint, with all the perseverance imaginable. The uneasiness they feel comes not only from the fact that they are dealing with a real pain in the neck, as the saying goes, someone who comes to bother them at the most inappropriate times. He is provoked even more deeply by a two-fold cause which it is important to be able to identify and situate.

The first cause is the fact that the desperate efforts of the partner's inner policeman are aimed directly at the accompanist's policeman. The former would like to affect the latter, wake it up if need be, and finally bring it around to its own scenario. It wants to associate it with its own task by asking it in turn to condemn the guilty person, to punish him if necessary or to acquit, to absolve him in order to relieve him for a brief instant of his torture. It goes without saying that, to the degree that the accompanist's exercise of discernment on his own inner policeman has not yet been given all the fruits of balance and peaceful distance that one might expect, the frontal attack he must face puts him in touch with his own weakness. He senses obscurely an attempt at manipulation on the still uncontrolled ground of his personality, trying to dictate sentiments and attitudes in him which informed simple common sense already condemns. The accompanist is subjected to an inner tension which causes great psychic distress. Without an *ad hoc* answer, the accompanist is seized with an almost irresistible urge to flee the scrupulous person and desert him by cutting the telephone off or barricading himself behind his office doors if necessary, if this were the only means left to him to escape falling under the scrupulous policeman's control.

The second cause of his discomfort is linked with the scrupulous person's attitude, which does not only aim at his accompanist's inner policeman. More specifically, through the latter's inner policeman he aims at a deeper level in his accompanist. But appearances to the contrary, the scrupulous person's cry is a request for love. Let us remember here that the inner policeman in each person crystallizes the traces his unconscious has kept of an authority's first interventions in his life. This is always a tenderly loved and absolutely vital authority—that of father or mother. The bond each person cultivates unconsciously with his inner policeman always includes a strongly affective component. We can even say that, strictly speaking, the scrupulous person is to a certain point in love with his inner policeman. The control he wants to exert on his accompanist is not unrelated to love. As strange as it may seem, the unconscious message given by the scrupulous person often goes so far as 'Punish me because you love me'. For some scrupulous people, whose inner policeman has taken on a particularly pervasive importance, there is, so to speak, no other loving word possible.

Such a message is obviously fundamentally ambiguous. Each accompanist will try to answer it by the means he has at hand at the moment, whatever they may be. For some, such a message will be fascinating and can become a trap into which they risk falling; for others, it will be literally unbearable and thus to be fled immediately at all costs.

How can we help a scrupulous person? A first method, which must be rejected right away, is the accompanist's temptation to expose his knowledge of the phenomenon to the victim without beating around the bush, proving to him by means of arguments that he presents an interesting case of the overdevelopment of the super-ego which habitually conditions the psychological makeup of the scrupulous person. This overview of the inner policeman's daily work would be of absolutely no use to the person involved! Spiritual accompaniment consists only very exceptionally in giving teaching or advice. It is first and foremost an experience lived and shared together.

To try to explain his policeman's malfunctioning to someone would be a new way of teaching him and charging his conscience. If he is scrupulous, he will think this is because something is not working right in him, and he is once more at fault. Generally, an interpretation like this will hurt the person concerned very deeply and so will be violently rejected. It offends his feelings, and even more his remaining self-esteem. Once this has happened, the relationship rarely can continue satisfactorily. From that point on, the person accompanied will be wary of his accompanist. He will even be tempted to burn his bridges to end what he can only feel was a painful misunderstanding, the entire responsibility for which he will place on his listener. Things have every chance of happening this way because it is true that what helps most of the time is not reasoning, even objectively correct reasoning. Only a progressive awareness of his desires, as well as the perversions and disguises they assume, can bring the light hoped for. Such coming to awareness is only rarely helped by communicating knowledge. One person can help another in this matter only indirectly by trying to facilitate the work of clarification he needs to do on himself. It is always up to him to catch himself red-handed or better still to catch his desires in the act of perversion and disguise.

Another classic way of helping a scrupulous person is calming him with words which are supposed to appease him. Some have been quoted above: 'This is not matter for sin; you were not fully free to consent; in any case, you didn't really want to offend God.' These words are objectively true. Literally speaking, they will do no harm. Experience has long ago shown that they have very little effect in appeasing the scrupulous person, or a very temporary effect. We spoke earlier about this kind of reaction which refuses to tackle the root of the problem. One of the reasons for its ineffectiveness is found in the fact that, in many cases, the scrupulous person does not desire fundamentally and sincerely to be healed of his handicap. As we have just recalled, displaying his anguish is often the only way he has left of beginning an even slightly affective relationship with a person near him. Why would he deprive himself of this bargain, which is his only means to salvation?

There is still another reason for the ineffectiveness of such a method. It was already mentioned, but we should study its validity by a concrete example. By trying to appease the scrupulous person this way, one occupies the very place of the inner policeman, taking over its job and gestures. One tries in doing so, of course, to deflect its speech in the direction one believes to be right: this person is not as guilty as he desperately believes. Instead of condemning him, one aims at acquitting him. The scrupulous person will be relieved, but only for a brief moment. As soon as the accompanist has turned his back and disappeared from the scene, the inner policeman, who here really deserves the name 'interior torturer', will qui-

etly return to its task. And the scene of torture will start
again as before, without end and, if need be, until despair.
No real opening to a solution is possible if one remains at the level of this policeman. This is even truer
in that the inner policeman occupies exactly that place
in this scruple-tormented depth where there should
arise the sweetness of the love of the Holy Spirit, which
Tradition calls repentance. In fact, what is truly at issue here is the qualitative passage from psychological
guilt, which occupies the whole conscience, more or
less, to the grace of repentance. Now as long as the
inner policeman can freely hold sway or its place is
clumsily occupied by the accompanist, even if he is inspired by the best of intentions, the way of repentance
is blocked, and without a miracle—which is always
possible—nothing truly salvific is going to happen.

Another common way to help the scrupulous person is
to suggest blind obedience to his spiritual Father. As an
emergency solution, this may be valuable, allowing the
strange behavior of some scrupulous persons to be cut
short and preventing them from ridicule in the eyes of
those around them. But this cannot take the place of true
therapy. The reason is simple: finding himself face to face
with a flesh and blood policeman who is a carbon copy of
his own interior policeman can only fulfill all the scrupulous person's unconscious wishes. This exterior presence
has a nature that will comfort and relieve him for an instant, when the inner tension is too great. It will not let
him advance one single step along the path to freedom.
Once again, the accompanist disguised as an exterior policeman will only confirm the one which continues to prevail within. This is a tranquilizer or a palliative, certainly
useful in many cases, but purely 'symptomatic', as they
say in medical language, meaning, it treats the symptoms
but does not address the deep causes.

How can one help the scrupulous person? Long, patient listening will progressively loosen the inner

policeman's hold and make it as evanescent, as null and void, as possible, allowing the Spirit's deep life to well up from within at the right time and little by little to take over this super-ego, to evangelize it and transform it. At the end of the process, this authority will no longer have the face of a policeman, it will have become 'interior anointing', *unctio magistra;* it will no longer be a Law, but Grace, flowing from the source, purely and simply.

Unfortunately, it is easier to describe the process abstractly than it is to put it into action. This, of course, is where the quality of the bond between accompanist and person accompanied is accentuated and can reveal itself as particularly effective. To the degree that the accompanist is truly quickened by this interior anointing and not subjected to the imperious injunctions of his policeman, something of this vital perception and contact will be transmitted, little by little as by a slow osmosis, to the experience of the person accompanied. And this, until the time when the quality of the bond of love and confidence between them is so great that it will counterbalance and even prevail over the unconscious bonds that enslave the latter to his interior policeman.

One sometimes hears this advice being recommended to be given to the scrupulous: 'Be at peace, because I am with you. I take on myself all the weight of your fault, if there is a fault, with all its consequences.' That someone agrees out of love, not only to walk beside him, but also to substitute for him in bearing the weight, can surely reach the other in his deepest need. Such a word is far more than a calming word which reassures temporarily. It takes the other seriously in his grief, with all the weight of his suffering, and agrees to bear it with him, simply out of love.

Such a sharing of wounds truly represents a crucial moment at the heart of the relationship of accompaniment. It is applicable, not only to the scrupulous, but any time a wound, a weakness or suffering are confided. Such shar-

ing goes beyond the scope of what is described in psycho-
therapy as empathy. This is an attitude of benevolent neutrality, and even what we, following Maurice Bellet, have
called the 'strange love' which manifests itself in listening
to the end. This sharing also goes further than simple
transfer, the elements of which, left to themselves, do not
have the transforming force needed to undermine the
other's resistance. Only the quickening bond which the
accompanist is able to establish with his own source in
the depths of his own being is capable of this. Now to
share another's suffering in a true love (and not, of course,
out of some obscure tendency to masochism) affects the
other in his deepest Centre, and is able to remove from
him all that prevents him from establishing contact with
his own interior source. In the case of the scrupulous person, it is a sharing of his false guilt, a sharing out of the
spiritual joy, the Spirit's anointing, by which the accompanist lives, which sometimes allows this guilt to be reduced and diluted. In this way an opening beyond the accompanied person's inner policeman allows access to his
own joy from which, in the Holy Spirit, a beginning of
authentic repentance can spring up. Only true repentance
in the Holy Spirit can definitively heal the scrupulous person.

This is, of course, the ideal solution, but unfortunately
it is an extreme case. In a large number of cases, in fact,
when certain facts bear too heavily on the situation, an
appreciable improvement is not very or not at all foreseeable, without a very special intervention by divine power.
In certain cases, a psychological improvement would not
be very desirable, because the person in question vitally
needs his scruples to defend himself against the awareness of certain things which, humanly speaking, would
otherwise be too heavy to bear. Even if this is the case, the
accompanist's capacity to listen remains a real and beneficial support, because the bond of confidence patiently
woven between him and the scrupulous person can com-

pensate to a certain degree for the ravages caused by the inner policeman. This fraternal gesture remains essential in all circumstances. Spiritual help is necessary here, as it is for every handicap and trial, so that the word which God speaks to all those who find themselves in such an apparently blocked situation can be discerned and interpreted.

If the person is still relatively young, one must not conclude too quickly that his scrupulous state is permanent. Time and patience, along with the accompanist's experience, can be very effective. But there are other cases where age, the formation received, and the solidity of the interior defenses indicate that one may reasonably conclude that the person in question will die with his scruples, or perhaps even will die of his scruples. That is no exaggeration. We meet cases where a scrupulous person, having finally used up all his energy resisting the oppressive weight of his anguish as well as he could, finally suffocated psychologically under this leaden weight and physically died of it. This is not an absolute evil: it is a death, as is any other. The important thing is that persons undergoing such trials be spiritually helped to see, through the burden of their guilt and anguish, some light of the Holy Spirit, who never ceases to work in them. Despite appearances, one must never doubt this work of the Spirit, and it is possible to glimpse unistakable signs of his work. In so apparently anguished a person, so incapable of correctly judging some detail of his behavior, there can in fact remain a zone of deep peace. Of course, this peace will not be apparent at first sight. The symptoms of anguish utterly dominate. Yet for someone who listens with his heart and his gut feeling, there soon appears this zone of peace, dominated by the trust of a very small child, particularly when the person himself is able to listen in the same way, especially at the time of prayer. It is at this level that the Holy Spirit works, and it is at this level that the person must be reached, confirmed and moved forward.

Then one must be very careful not to extinguish this childlike confidence by good advice which would only resurrect and replace the inner policeman's reproaches. One would instantly change the level of intervention and might run the risk of taking away from this person his only remaining hope of breathing a little, despite the scruples that he never stops dwelling on and despite the evil he believes he is committing. More than ever, one must refuse the temptation of helping him by taking the place of the inner policeman. Once again, this is not easy. The temptation is often strong, and before even being aware of it the accompanist is already taking the policeman's place, forestalling any possibility of helping that person deeply. To refuse this temptation obstinately, and not yield to the other's policeman, sometimes seems like hand-to-hand combat. Let us beware of imagining that this is a combat in which we might triumph by brute force, even though it could possibly happen that our dreams, unfettered by the requirements of discernment, may compensate for the frustrations born of restraint by giving free rein to violent scenes in which, for example, one bests the other by wringing his neck. The other in question would probably be a symbol of the policeman, that is, one's own policeman rather than the other person's!

On the contrary, gentleness acts in the accompanist. This gentleness is his most interior strength, springing up from the deepest part of himself. This is in all truth the anointing of the Holy Spirit which every baptized person has received in his heart. Thanks to this quality of being, everything in him and in the relationship will be beneficial to the other— the silences and the words, his presence and his absence—because everything which springs from true love is able to restore and heal, to build a new person who can thenceforth be reborn, not from the distortions and anguish of his false guilt, but from the sweetness of the tears of repentance. Before speaking of repentance, this crucial object of spiritual accompaniment, we must take a look at another trap in spiritual dialogue: the mirror, in which man takes pleasure in contemplating a God in his image and likeness, the image of what he believes himself obliged to be.

To illustrate the actions of the interior policeman in a different way, let us reread two sayings which come down from ancient monastic literature. It goes without saying that this literature was unaware of the concept of superego or the policeman image. The discernment which it proposes shows several times over how conscious the ancient monks were of the ravages caused by feelings of guilt which have nothing in common with true repentance.

This is the first saying:

> At the devil's instigation, a brother who lived in the solitary desert often fell into the sin of lust. But he never ceased doing violence to himself not to leave the monastic life, and, praying his modest office, he prayed to God with groaning and said: 'Lord, whether I will it or whether I do not will it, save me, because I who am ashes love sin, but you, Almighty God, prevent me. It is not a great thing if you have mercy on the just, and there is nothing admirable if you save the pure, because they are worthy of mercy. But in me, Master, manifest your mercy, and for this show your love towards man, because the poor man abandons himself to you.' This is what he used to say all the time, whether he had fallen or not. Now, when he had fallen and given in to his most deeply-rooted vice, he got up immediately and began the office of prayer. But the devil, astonished at his confidence and his boldness, appeared to him and said: 'How can you not blush to stand before God

and pronounce his Name when you recite
the psalms?' The brother replied: 'I swear to
you by the Name of the One who came to
save sinners by calling them to penance, I
will not stop praying God against you, as long
as you have not stopped warring against me.
And we will see who will win, you or God.'
At these words, the devil said to him: 'Surely,
now I will no longer war against you, so that
I will not obtain a crown for you by your
patience." This is how patience is good, patience that does not become discouraged even
if we often fall in our struggles, sins and temptations.'[1]

The brother in this saying seems already to have an experience of repentance. The prayer he addresses to the
Lord after his falls expresses it perfectly. He is harassed,
however, by another voice within, whispering to him, in
vain, that, in the state in which he finds himself, he should
be ashamed to pray. The brother will not yield because he
is too certain of God's mercy. The most significant thing
about this text is the fact that the saying attributes to the
devil the voice which some might have been tempted to
identify with the 'voice of conscience'. The saying attributes
it correctly. It is obviously the guilt-inducing voice of the
inner policeman, whose tone the devil knows very well
how to imitate to discourage the sinner. The resolute way
in which this monk long ago succeeded in outwitting the
trap is utterly remarkable.

Here is another saying in the same vein. Let us first read
it all:

A brother lived in the monastery of soli-
tudes and his prayer was always as follows:

1. Lucien Regnault, *Les Sentences des Pères du Désert. Nouveau recueil,
apophtegmes inédits ou peu connus* (Solesmes 1970) N582.

'Lord, I do not have the fear of you, but send me lightning, or another calamity, or an illness, or a devil, so that at least in this way my insensitive soul will learn to fear you.' And he also prayed to God saying: 'Master, if it is possible, in your mercy forgive me, and if that is not possible, chastise me in this life, Master, but not in the next.' He continued thus to moan all the time. One day when he was sitting on the ground, exhausted and discouraged, he fell asleep. And Christ came to him and said to him with a happy countenance and a happy tone of voice: 'What is the matter, brother? Why are you crying?' He said to him: 'Because I have fallen, Lord.' The apparition said to him: 'Well then, get up!' He who was on the ground answered: 'I cannot unless you give me your hand'. And the Lord held out his hand to him, lifted him up and said to him still cheerfully: 'Why are you crying, brother, why are you troubled?' The brother said: 'Do you not agree, Lord, that I be troubled, since I have given you so much trouble?' Then the apparition stretched out his hand and put his palm on the brother's head. The brother at last took his hand and the apparition said to him: 'Do not be distressed. God comes to your help: from now on since you have been troubled, I will no longer be troubled about you; if because of you I have given my blood, how much more will I give my mercy to any soul who repents.' And coming to himself, the brother found his heart full of joy.[2]

2. Regnault, *Sentences,* N583.

The meaning of this saying, at first a little complicated, is just as transparent. We must not be led astray by the two prayer formulas at the beginning of the story, which at first sight seem strange. They are simply bad prayers. They spring, not from the Holy Spirit, but from the interior policeman and the discouragement he constantly inspires. The first prayer is a request the monk makes to God: to obtain the fear of God. With fear as his goad, the supplicant would in future be more virtuous, that is, strong against himself, and in this state would fulfill all the rules under the eyes of 'God'. The second request is as badly inspired: since God's justice is what it is, it is better to receive the reward of his faults by present evils than in the future life. It is because man is reduced to powerlessness that 'God' is living by the rules of his own justice. There is no question of mercy in either prayer.

No one can be misled about the identity of the one who judges the degree of fault and establishes the barometer of reparation. These 'Make me afraid', 'Do evil to me', and in either case 'Make me fulfill the rules', are so many echoes sent back to their source: the inner policeman.

In the theme's development, the saying tries to show the crumbling of his omnipotence as his interior glance is enlightened. The guilt-inducing attitude is worn away by its own persuasive force: nature yields, overwhelmed. The brother falls asleep. In a dream he reaches down to the depth of his soul, which has remained healthy, and he discovers that he is redeemed and not a being possessed by the demon of his quasi-destitution.

What was death-bearing has become a pretext for grace. In its very weakness, the weight of overburdened nature causes it to implode to its center. In this sense, mercy precedes and overflows our theological narrowness, carrying us along irresistibly in an inner revolution. There this impulse of the heart takes shape, in the passivity of its breaking which is at the same time its most extreme activity.

Yet the hidden well of the tears of repentance is unsealed only by the effect of grace, set free in person by a Word or a teaching which announces it and is its fruit. Reflected in this pool is the image of a man reunified in love and not caged up by justice –and what a justice— within his centrifugal desires.

Unlike the policeman, the only interior Master does not judge, condemn, or chastise. On the contrary, he raises the sinner up, embraces, and consoles him: 'How much more will I give my mercy to any soul who repents.' This is true repentance, which floods the forgiven sinner with joy. Without being able to name it, but with uncanny accuracy, this marvelous example of spiritual discernment has already identified the inner authority which psychology much later was to call the super-ego, and which the Evil One has always known how to use only too well.

TWO INNER AUTHORITIES: 7
The MIRROR

EACH PERSON BEARS within himself a-
nother authority which, often without his knowledge, governs a significant part of his behavior.
Let us call it 'the inner mirror'. The mirror theme has an
illustrious past in greek mythology: Narcissus fell in love
with his reflection in the waters of a fountain; in it he
drowned, trying in vain to embrace his image. More recently, in psychoanalysis, there has been a renewed theo-
retical interest in the theme of mirror with the school of
Jacques Lacan.

The interior mirror is not unrelated to the experience
everybody has when, for the first time, he perceives his
own image in a mirror placed in front of him (the 'stage
of the mirror', Lacan calls it). Contemplating an image
from which he is separated by the distance between himself and the mirror, he apprehends himself as 'me': an experience of identity–It's me!–in otherness and rift–the
mirror is other than me; it is outside me. From then on, in
each interpersonal encounter, each subject will try to find
his own image in the eyes of the other. He will want to
appear lovable and loved in the other's eyes. This is the
fascinating and cruelly frustrating experience of the phenomenon of love—to cite only this universally known example. Indeed, in this other person, completely reflected
in the first image and reduced to this image, each person
can temporarily meet only his own emotions and his own
satisfaction, appropriately called 'narcissistic'. The phenomenon of love does not yet affect the other person in
himself. True love is still very far away: the other person in
his difference is not reached at all.

The subject does not put off introducing into himself

this mirror-image of himself by reconstructing it within himself. Very quickly, too, he will need constantly to embellish it, to be ever more lovable in the eyes of those he meets and in this way tries to seduce. This embellishment will be done according to the criteria of approval or confirmation which the subject thinks he reads in other people's eyes. It goes without saying that it is here, in the progressive development of this mirror, that the inner policeman, along with everything he forbids or permits, plays a considerable role. In this way, every subject, little by little, builds up an ideal or idealized self—like a mirror in which he contemplates himself and by which feels approved by himself and others.

This mirror, which at first functions only at the level of primary emotions, will at length foster an ideal of life, a schema of perfection, even an ideology or philosophy. Any 'ideal', whatever its undeniable respectability may be, has some link with the interior mirror, a link which is not necessarily negative. The 'ideal' of christian or religious life does not escape this subtle connivance. It is important for us to know this to diminish the ever possible risk of reducing a vocation to this pleasing narcissistic mirror in which someone likes to admire himself still more, at the risk of drowning.

Our image of God can also be affected by the inner mirror to the degree that we may project our idealized self into the place of God and innocently exchange this, elevated to maximum perfection, for our own mirror. It is obvious that the true God would have no part in this false image, which would be only an idol, one more idol! We may remember that the inner policeman can also hold the place of an idol, usurping the true God's place. Once again, one of the purposes of spiritual accompaniment is precisely to liberate us from such false gods.

But before freeing us from this idol, accompaniment will aim at freeing us from ourselves by making us autonomous over against this mirror. In fact, by turning our

attention towards an illusion, the mirror and the policeman both keep us from our deep reality, which is at the
same time our true desires and the Spirit's anointing in
us. In the case of the policeman, the illusion is a tyranni-
cal authority reducing us to slavery; as for the mirror, the
illusion is a imposing ideal whose brilliance blinds us to
our real condition. In both cases, the artifice aims to con-
ceal wounds which the unconscious judges too painful
to be faced.

Someone may object here: unlike the inner policeman,
could this mirror not be used positively in accompaniment? The policeman exercised a repressive, disparaging
and depressing influence. The mirror, on the contrary,
seems at first sight able to revitalize the subject towards a
promising future. This objection can be answered in a few
words. In the short term, yes, maybe. This dynamic will
not have a long term impact. On the contrary, because the
ideal the mirror reflects to us and holds out to our partner, or even to God, does not correspond at all with what
we are and can do in reality. The mirror's role consists
precisely in concealing unbearable weaknesses. In a certain sense, we might even say that every 'ideal', whatever
it may be, lay, humanist, or religious, easily lets itself be
turned away from its own purpose by any person, becoming for him a consolation prize and a compensation for
his weaknesses. The ideal gives a person the illusion of
being able to become someone he really is not, and allows
him to refuse the person he, in fact, is. In everything he
does, the subject is constantly tempted to judge himself in
relation to the image the mirror reflects to him. This 'oblique glance', by which someone constantly compares himself to the ideal reflected by his mirror, is typical of the
narcissistic attitude. But when referred to an illusion, the
ideal holds the subject in the illusion that he can do without the only awareness that matters.

Not that any ideal or ideology would necessarily play
such a negative role. On the contrary, their regulatory func-

tion is not without importance within a given culture and so too within the religious culture. Their influence becomes perverse only to the degree that, within accompaniment, a person tries to ask them for a service they cannot give. They run the risk of cutting the subject off from his deep desires, which are fiercely real and which will not agree for long to be thus generously immolated to the narcissistic mirror's profit.

The oblique glance toward the inner mirror is perfectly illustrated by a saying of Saint Anthony. For him, prayer is not perfect as long as the person praying is still conscious of praying, that is, occupied in bringing to mind from time to time the outline of the ideal prayer his mirror reflects to him, to compare it with his own prayer. To pray truly is always to overflow from within, despite oneself, and not to be curbed by a model of prayer to which we conform, no matter what.

If the narcissistic image can play this disturbing role in spiritual experience, prudence is all the more appropriate in the course of spiritual accompaniment, where each of the two interlocutors bears an inner mirror. To the degree that the dialogue of accompaniment leads to the reciprocal confrontation of these two mirrors, it would evidently remain sterile; the mirror is there precisely only as a screen between the subjects and their desires. This risk will be all the greater when both partners in the dialogue belong to the same spiritual family whose identity is clearly perceived and strongly affirmed—which is usually the case in a monastery or a religious family.

One of the first needs the person accompanied experiences when he approaches his accompanist is to hold his inner mirror out to him in the barely concealed goal of having him approve it. Of course, he does this without announcing it explicitly and often even without being aware of it. From the very first meeting, however, it is relatively easy to discern the main features of the idealized image inscribed in this mirror. The person makes known the aspects he judges positive and those he judges negative by the fears   which he alludes to, the failings he accuses himself of, or accuses others of. This mirror held out to the accompanist is truly a trap. There is nothing easier or more gratifying for both than to fall innocently into it. By congratulating him when the person accompanied seems to score points relative to his ideal, or by multiplying the reproaches when he admits himself deficient, the accompanist uses all his know-how to favor the mirror and its perverse effects. The only contribution, and it is hardly positive, he might make in this way would be in adjusting and fine-tuning the ideal with the goal of making it more in keeping with certain evangelical norms, for instance. This work would not be useless, of course, but it would bring about only an increase of knowledge, without reaching the deep level of desires, which is the only important level and the place of growth within dialogue. The risk is great that, without their knowing it, the two dialogue partners tend to be in agreement very quickly about what the ideal to be pursued should be. There is nothing more reassuring for the person accompanied than to recognize his own mirror in his guide's approving words.

The tragic aspect of the situation, as we have seen above, is that such a reassuring mirror prevents the subject from going deeper into himself, to the level of his true desires and,one may add, to the level where the Holy Spirit—that is, the desire or love of God for him—is at work in him, and does not cease urging him, as Saint Paul used to say *(2 Cor 5:14; Gal 5:16-18)*. The pedagogical method used by God always goes in exactly the opposite direction from a reinforcement or embellishment of the mirror. God forever manages to break the mirror, to free up the inner path which leads to the true self. A correct accompaniment, far from keeping up with and encouraging the mirror, should therefore be content with waiting patiently for the critical moment in human experience— still more in spiritual experience—when the mirror will break. At this decisive moment in the person's journey, the quality of the presence of the one accompanying him will have an incalculable bearing.

We have said that it is fitting that the accompanist wait for the mirror to break—at least, as a general rule. Some accompanists may perhaps be tempted to break it themselves. A word, a gesture or an attitude could rush things. But in most cases, such an initiative would have as disastrous an effect as that caused by a misplaced word, as we saw in the case of the inner policeman's authority. Yet it can happen that the situation has matured enough and both partners feel ready enough to face such an incident and bear the consequences. Above all, however, one must not presume anything and must act only very advisedly, because in most cases this violent action is not called for. We need only wait for the mirror to break by itself. Life is of itself strong enough to take over and to prevent someone from being deluded indefinitely. And what can we say about the force of life which is the Holy Spirit! Once again, God's whole pedagogical method and the divine cunning he uses have as a goal this breaking of the mirror and its illusions, which will happen sooner or later.

Sacred History contains several examples of this divine pedagogical method. One of the most revealing is no doubt the case of Saint Paul. The inner mirror in which he long took pleasure is transparent in the claims to nobility he still recited when, in what he described as a moment of folly, he contemplated himself in his mirror discreetly to derive some glory from it: 'Circumcised on the eighth day, of the race of Israel, of the tribe of Benjamin, a Hebrew of hebrew parentage, in observance of the law a Pharisee, in zeal I persecuted the church, in righteousness based on the law I was blameless' *(Phil 3:5-6).*

Something decisive happened in the life of Saint Paul; an event opened the way to his deep heart, allowing him to count all of that as a negligible loss when compared to the knowledge of Jesus Christ. This event illustrates eloquently and colorfully the breaking of a mirror: that of judaic perfection. Its weight had become so unbearable to his fervor, although it was exemplary, that Paul was later to repeat constantly that such perfection is incapable of freeing man and giving him life.

The example of Paul illustrates this anterior event of which we have already spoken: Christ's appearing causes a physical as well as spiritual upheaval. The picture of Paul's distress on the road to Damascus is especially striking: the man is hurled to the ground, called out to, reduced to the condition of a man wandering in darkness. This state includes the mystery of the time of conversion which accompanies God's breaking in. The event provides the occasion for an inward journey by teaching and sacrament. Having recovered his sight through the prayer of one of those he had persecuted before his inner conversion, Paul received baptism at the end of eight days. Three long years in the desert followed; a time when he grew stronger in his new faith, progressively adjusting to his new situation as convert at the same time as he stopped mourning the first mirror image of zealot-for-the-Law. From this spiritual and ecclesial teaching method was to arise the word of freedom in the Spirit—witness Paul's renewal which he proclaimed from then on—at odds with his previous certainties and acts, and in which his former companions would never have recognized the former zealot.

The movement of breaking this judaic mirror corresponds to that instant where Paul, on the ground, heard himself addressed in such a way that he did not recognize the secret name of the person doing it: Jesus. It was a radical change into newness. Paul had just lost his unconscious psychological foothold, swept away by an irresistible force. He had to relearn the face of his deep self. Everything became possible: he was no longer anything in his own eyes, and the landmarks for which other people's eyes were the refuge were reduced to nothing.

Paul owed the knowledge of his deep self to the shattering of his mirror. From then on he could take the path of truth about himself, a road to deep reconciliation which distanced itself unambiguously from any tension towards the ideal he had constructed. Paul truly found himself in his dizzying weakness. Confronted with his authentic self, where there was no more flattering image, Paul reached the depths of his original condition as creature in a question posed to his Lord. Later, he was to confess the mystery of this weakness quickened by grace, in this wonderful hymn from the second Letter to the Corinthians: 'I will glory in my weakness . . . My grace is sufficient for you . . ., because my strength is made manifest in weakness . . . It is when I am weak that I am strong' *(2 Cor 12:17)*—a hymn which could only spring from the shards of his broken mirror and in the assurance and the vow of bearing fruit only in the constant company of the Lord and in his sight, in the liberating power of Jesus' name. Without the presence and gaze of Jesus, in fact, Paul would never have been able to get through such a trial unscathed.

Paul's dazzling vocation must put the accompanist on his guard about the effects of the mirror's shards. For anyone who for many years has practiced conforming his life to the features reflected in the mirror, reassuring himself by sideways glances to it from time to time or caught by the accompanist's words in this mirror's power of attraction, for this person to be suddenly deprived of his mirror is comparable only to the general disruption produced by an earthquake. It is a deep upheaval which cannot avoid producing a weight of anguish: everything becomes unrecognizable. To speak figuratively: the scenery and the contours of the land have been changed. The plains rise, becoming hills, and the mountains are laid low, becoming flat ground. From now on, nothing will be the same as it was before. First, all the securities of the person become unworkable, the ground gives way under his feet, he has the impression of being swept up, unhinged, not knowing even where he will land and what anchorage will be his then.

Such upheaval is not without risk. It can so radically affect the structures of the subject that it can lead him to the last frontier of his psychological equilibrium, to the limit of possible madness. One must not be astonished or panic-stricken at this. In every spiritual maturation such a moment can arrive sooner or later. The life of the Spirit is able to transform our inner structures so deeply that, before yielding to this spiritual *aggiornamento,* they come dangerously close to collapsing, generally when the subject's ego is quite particularly fragile. The risk is never totally dispelled. If the subject succeeds in safeguarding his psychological integrity during such a trial, he owes this to the revelation of God's mercy, made to him at the heart of this experience. Only an infinite love shown to him at so crucial a moment can reconcile him with himself, with the pieces of his mirror, and with the ruins of his ideal of perfection.

The role of the spiritual guide, in such circumstances, is obviously of the greatest importance. He will be the first sign of God and the saving hand of his grace, and be aided in this by the quality of his relationship with the person accompanied, right down to the tact necessary to outwit the pitfalls of transferential identifications. Another attitude could be envisaged for him: either to try patiently to reassemble the scattered pieces and reconstitute the mirror; or propose his own mirror as a compensating substitution. Consoling or reassuring in this way can, in fact, only prevent from happening what could finally have happened! Once the mirror is broken, a path is opened to the deep core of one's being and one's true nobility. This is never to be seen in the mirror, however shiny it may be, but it is found at the deepest level of the heart, where God waits to welcome the subject in crisis. It is therefore by the quality of his spiritual life, his contact with his own deep center, that the accompanist is active in this crisis, his very presence laden with love, transparent like the clear mirror wherein the image of the consoling and redeeming God is reflected effectively by his Word, his look, his mercy. So great is the distance which separates the mirror's psychology and games from the mystery of the icon lying hidden in the depths of being, a mystery of charity. In the depths of the other's eyes—this other person who takes charge of him in love—the person accompanied can recognize a reflection of what awaits him in the depth of his own heart: he is forgiven by infinite mercy and he finds there the source of infinite freedom.

At the heart of such a relationship, any word spoken by the accompanist must be carefully, lovingly weighed. The chance, and the risk, are that any word can be terribly effective. Above all else, this word must come, not from the head or some good feelings, but truly from the deepest part of his being, from the Lord present in the speaker. One single word will then be amply sufficient, the right word, spoken at the right time, with the right inflection. In such a case we may sense the degree to which a simple human word can in turn be creative, restorative, vivifying—as the Word of God always is. The word of a spiritual father is truly able to beget in his son the New Man in Jesus Christ.

THE GRACE OF REPENTANCE

Getting as adroitly as possible around the harmful influences of the inner policeman or mirror opens the way for true repentance and allows a person thereafter to distinguish it from false guilt or the false ideals which so often ravage spiritual experience. This is why true repentance in the Holy Spirit is the touchstone of all authentically christian spiritual experience. It is also the first criterion of discernment. To this, it is appropriate to allude briefly.

Saint Isaac the Syrian, great monk and mystic of the

seventh century, describes the grace of christian repentance this way:

> Anyone who knows his sins is greater than someone who by his prayer raises a dead person . . . Anyone who groans for himself for an hour is greater than someone who teaches the whole universe. Anyone who knows his own weakness is greater than someone who sees the angels . . . Anyone who, alone and contrite, follows Christ, is greater than someone who enjoys the favor of the crowds in the churches.[1]

By these terms—which deliberately come close to paradox—Saint Isaac chose to highlight the specifically christian character of repentance. We meet repentance only in the wake of the Gospel, nowhere else, in no other religion and no other humanism. Christian repentance is reducible or comparable to no other experience of man left to his own strength. It cannot be counterfeit without risking ridicule or falling into imbalance. It is an absolutely sure fruit of the Holy Spirit and one of the clearest signs of his action in the soul.

The fact is that within each person repentance can spring up only from the shards of the inner mirror and once his account with the inner policeman has been settled. Psychology helps us in this way better to situate the source and meaning of repentance, as distinct from certain elemental psychological reactions which free us from feelings of remorse and give rise to reproaches of conscience which are not the fruit of a direct intervention of the Holy Spirit.

In this area, spiritual people of all time, despite their unavoidable ignorance of psychological data familiar to us today, continue to surprise us. Armed with an uncannily sure discernment—the fruit of the Holy Spirit in them,

---

1. *Discourse*, 34.

they were almost always able to distinguish between an
entirely exterior humility which is simply constraint, and
another humility which flows from the source and is the
ripe fruit of authentic love. Similarly, they were careful
not to confuse the repentance which springs from fear
and can only double fear, with a repentance that looses
tears which are not so much tears of pain as—and at the
same time—tears of joy and love.

Among spiritual persons whose discernment was
coupled with a remarkable psychological perceptiveness,
we may note among many others, Fénelon, Archbishop
of Cambrai towards the end of the seventeenth century.
The following text of his, without being able to name them,
dispels in advance the mirror's artifices and the policeman's
gesticulations:

> Only Jesus Christ can give us this true humility of heart
> which comes from him; it is born of the anointing of
> his grace. It does not consist, as one might imagine, in
> exterior acts of humility, although this is good, but in
> remaining in one's place. Someone who considers him-
> self something is not truly humble; someone who
> wants something for himself is not either. It is the per-
> son who forgets himself so much that he never thinks
> of himself, who is not turned in on himself, who is
> only lowliness within, who is not wounded by any-
> thing without affecting patience outwardly, who talks
> about himself as someone would talk about another,
> who does not affect forgetting himself when he is full
> of himself; who gives himself to charity without pay-
> ing attention whether doing so is humility or pride,
> who is quite content to pass for a person without hu-
> mility . . . We always tend to be something; we often
> make noise in devotion after having made noise in the
> things we have left behind. Why? Because we want to
> be noticed in every sort of state. But someone who is
> humble seeks nothing; to be humble or despised is all

the same to him because he does not take anything for himself and he lets them do anything they wish with him. There are many persons who practice exterior humility and who are very far from this humility of heart I have just described. The more a person thinks he is humbling himself, the more he is persuaded of his elevation. Anyone who notices that he is humbling himself [this is the oblique glance into the mirror!] is not yet in his place, which is below any self-abasement. The persons who believe they are humbled are very proud; and so deep down this sort of humility is often a subtle seeking after elevation. These sorts of humility will not enter into heaven without being reduced to pure charity, the source of the true humility, the only humility worthy of God and which he takes pleasure in filling with himself.[2]

Faking humility is impossible, Fénelon reminds us, as is faking repentance. Saint Bernard also distinguishes between two kinds of humility. A first kind is the fruit of objective reasoning: it comes out of necessity and without heat, he reminds us. A second kind, which springs from love, is spontaneous and warm and experiences no difficulty in letting itself be drawn into an effectively humble and despised situation. The first is only 'extorted' by a reasoning–*extorsit discussio veritatis*–, the second is insinuated by an inner touch of the heart–*cordis suasit affectio*.[3]

In several places, Bernard has no hesitation in describing the successive steps of spiritual experience or prayer as a progression in the quality of a person's view of his own sin, a constant evolution and purification of the feeling of guilt which accompanies it. Beginners experience only fear and trembling before a God, whom they still

---

2. *Instructions et avis sur divers points de la morale et de la perfection chrétienne*, published in François Varillon, *Fénélon et le pur amour* (Paris, 1957) 165 ff.
3. SC 42. 6-7.

know only as a severe judge; they are therefore reduced to getting irritable and angry at the sinners they are. Those who are making progress have already tasted something of the mercy of God; they no longer hesitate to plead with him confidently and fervently. Then come the 'perfect'—rare today, even among monks,Bernard confesses—those who overflow with a prophetic spirit and who like David and Peter 'easily get up again even after great falls' because they are already established in the simplicity of God who is their joy. 'Even if they fall from time to time, they do not think that God is angry; on the contrary, they judge that all things work together for their good, and they get up again stronger than before.' So certain are they of mercy that their prayer to obtain forgiveness for their sins is only an anticipated thanksgiving. *Gratiarum actio est de peccatis et de percipiendis, laus in Deum et benedictio :* thanksgiving for the sin and for the pardon to be received, praise to God and benediction. The formula is daring, but Bernard speaks no doubt from experience. To use the vocabulary we have, we would say that, in the saints, the inner policeman has given way to the sweetness and anointing of the inner Master, the Holy Spirit, who teaches us everything and who is sufficient for everything[4]

---

4. *Sententiae,* 3.101 and 3.124; [CF 55:330f, 433ff] cf. *Sermo de Diversis,* 25.

BEING FATHER *and/or* MOTHER 8

IN MADAGASCAR, every religious or civil high official receives the title *Raïnmandren*, literally 'Father and Mother'. This vocabulary testifies to a profound intuition about the exercise of authority. It has to do with firmness and gentleness, strength and tenderness. In his Rule, Saint Benedict also distinguishes a double personality in an abbot by attributing to each abbot different and complementary sentiments. The abbot is Father, and under this title he is endowed with a *pius affectus,* a sense of tenderness; but he is also Master and consequently must at the same time show a *durus affectus,* firmness or even harshness *(RB 2.24).* Saint Benedict does not, we notice, use maternal symbolism, but replaces 'father' with 'master' and 'mother' with 'father'. The substitution no doubt hints at what Benedict's personal psychology was, but it also suggests which sentiment will predominate–rightly or wrongly–in the exercise of abbatial authority. So, curiously for Benedict ,the paternal side of authority is first of all a maternal side: the abbot 'will see to it that mercy prevails over judgment' *(RB 64.10),* without denying the two complementary aspects he knew of the exercise of authority: firmness and gentleness.

Saint Benedict was not innovating. Long before him, Saint Paul, in the exercise of his own ministry, had not hesitated to apply to himself the images of father and mother with amazing psychological insight, attaching them respectively to one or another aspect of his ministry. The First Letter to the Thessalonians, perhaps the oldest work of Paul and of the New Testament, already presents a fairly complete little synthesis of this subject. Think of the context of this letter. Between Paul and his correspon-

141

dents there were some misunderstandings. He is now taking up the pen, he tells them, because he wants to point
out the rights he has acquired in relation to them. The
young christian church in Thessalonika had been founded
by him; therefore Paul believes he has some right to intervene firmly in the life of this community, even from a distance. To justify himself, he begins to describe the way he
used to act with them *(1 Thes 2:7-14)*. His attitude was
gentle and at the same time firm. He surrounded the
Thessalonians with his full affection, to the point of being accused of easy-going weakness, but at the same time
his word was firm and clear, giving very specific directions. This is how he presents himself:

> although we were able to impose our
> weight as an apostle of Christ . . . we were
> instead gentle among you, as a mother
> nurtures her children. So great was our
> affection for you that we were determined
> to share with you not only the gospel of
> God, but our very selves as well, so dearly
> beloved had you become to us.

He goes on to describe his toil, the combats of his
apostolate day and night in the service of his Thessalonians.
And he continues:

> As you know, we treated each one of you
> as a father treats his children, exhorting
> and encouraging you and insisting that you
> conduct yourselves as worthy of the God
> who calls you into his kingdom and glory.

Paul begins by comparing himself to a mother. In fact, the
greek word he uses here, *trophos,* means 'nurse'. At that
time, especially in some circles, the mother often lived at
some distance from her children and gave a wet-nurse

the job of nursing them. If Paul preferred the word 'nurse', no doubt he wanted to underscore the 'nursing' role of apostolic ministry. He goes so far as to compare the Good News of the Kingdom to milk, doesn't he? A little further on in the same Letter, in fact, he mentions the 'milk of the Gospel' *(1 Cor 3:2)*. Then we come on the verb *thalpein,* which is translated 'to surround with care', but this is almost not saying enough. The greek word is more expressive: 'to make a fuss over', 'to warm', 'to pamper', or even 'to overprotect'. The same is true for the greek word rendered 'so great an affection for you: *omeiromenoi,* a rare word, difficult to translate. It indicates a strong, languorous, almost pathological fondness. Paul seems to be confessing that, like a mother, he was dazzled and blinded by his affection for his dear Thessalonians. Like a mother, not only did he nourish his children with his own substance, but he would still be ready to give his life for them.

A few lines later Paul sees himself instead 'as a father' to his children. He worked hard for them, with his own hands, to enable him to proclaim the Gospel freely. And Paul details this aspect of his ministry, using specifically paternal images: exhorting, encouraging, insisting that you conduct yourselves as worthy of God. This is the father who makes his entrance and for an instant snatches the child from the mother's knees and breast to fling him into daily life. In any case, from the very beginning of his apostolic life, Paul was conscious of the fact that his method of teaching faith and spiritual experience called upon both the father and mother in him.

Other pauline texts will clarify both images. The image of mother is complemented in *Gal 4:19.* The Galatians, just like the Thessalonians, were no picnic for Paul. He had no more than turned his back on them after a first visit than they let themselves be swayed by other missionaries whose gospel differed from his. His heart suffered so much on this account that he compared his sufferings to those of a new birth: 'My little children, for whom I am again in labor until Christ be formed in you!' Thanks be to God, the apostle's sufferings were to be fruitful, he hoped, as is every mother's suffering, through which a new being comes into the world.

In the *First Letter to the Corinthians 4:14-16,* Paul specifies what the paternity he exercised towards them consists in. He had a brush with the Christians of Corinth trying to appease the rivalries revealed after his departure. At one point, his pen slipped a little and he showed his harsh side. To justify this harshness, he appeals to his quality of father. Other missionaries were merely guides for the Corinthians. Only Paul is their true father in Christ: 'I am writing you this not to shame you, but to admonish you as my beloved children. Even if you should have countless guides to Christ, yet you do not have many fathers, for I became your father in Christ Jesus through the gospel. Therefore, I urge you, be imitators of me.' We hear the outpouring of fatherly feelings: Paul exhorts and corrects. More than that: he urges the Corinthians to imitate him, as sons experience a need to identify with their father and act as he does. He specifies also how he became their father: the seed of his paternity is the Word of God, the Gospel, which Paul alone planted in their hearts. It is because of the Word of the Gospel that Paul can say in all truth that he has begotten the Corinthians to life in Christ Jesus. Saint Peter recalls this in his First Letter *(1:23)*: 'You have been born anew, not from perishable but from imperishable seed, through the living and abiding Word of God.'

What is important for us in these texts is that Paul did not hesitate to place himself in the paternal and maternal roles at the same time. The Apostle, and after him the spiritual accompanist, participates in a divine function because he is in the image of God and God is always both father and mother at the same time. Infinitely father and 'more than father', as the poet said; infinitely mother and 'more than mother'. This is why Paul never hesitated to go from one to the other, almost without transition. He pleads like a mother and a few verses later threatens like a father.

This double image of the father and the mother tells us something very deep both about God and about human beings. That we are led to say that God is both father and mother reveals to us *a posteriori* the difficulty God must have felt—if we may express ourselves so anthropomorphically—when, in creating human beings in his image and likeness, he had to distinguish and to reunite what was united in him. The image of God incarnate in humanity and living among men was, as it were, obliged to split in two. Only man and woman, simultaneously and complementarily, could translate a little more adequately the inconceivable richness of the mystery of communion, communication, exchange, and union in God. This is particularly true when it comes to his love, with its double component of tenderness and strength. The Bible always carefully distinguishes them while uniting them in one and the same formula. God is at the same time *hesed* and *emet, misericordia* and *veritas,* tenderness and faithfulness. Translated to humanity and human language, the love of God was to give birth to two complementary beings and vocabularies, equally human and at the same time profoundly different: man and woman and their mutual affective richness. Man, witness and sign of God's strength and solidity; woman, witness and sign of his gentleness, his infinite welcome. One single human being would not have been enough: human nature had to be two, and two in one. From then on all divine and human pedagogy is based on the fruitful complementarity of these 'two in one'. As the text of Genesis already insinuated: 'God created man in his image, male and female he created them' *(Gn 1:27).*

The male on his part is *Emet,* fidelity, or rather, solidity, firmness, made in the image of the solidity and firmness of God. We can lean on God as on a rock which will not yield. We can build on him as on a foundation which will not fail. In woman, the human being is also *Hesed,* that is, infinite tenderness, always there to welcome and forgive. That God can be infallibly strong, even when he shows himself tender and merciful is, from our point of view, one of the most surprising and the most inconceivable aspects of his mystery. As long as we have not truly met God but know only the ideas or convictions we have devised about him, as long as we have not, literally, bumped into him, we cannot picture to ourselves how such a strength can go hand in hand with such a tenderness— we are almost tempted to say: with such a weakness. The collect for the Twenty-sixth Sunday in Ordinary Time says it marvelously: *Deus qui omnipotentiam tuam parcendo maxime et miserando manifestas:* God who show your almighty power especially in your mercy and forgiveness. This marvel belongs specifically to God and it is, in a certain sense, inimitable. And this is what complicates things for a human being who is called to hold the place of God, whether as leader or accompanist at the heart of spiritual dialogue.

In family life in a normally constituted home, that is, where the father and the mother are adequately present and play their part more or less correctly, things are a little simpler. As we have seen, the image of God is reflected in the complementary action of both. The father can show himself strict and even severe while the mother's goodness provides adequate counterbalance. And the mother can show herself almost excessively good when she can count on the father for the indispensable calls to order. It goes without saying that one more condition is required: the affective harmony of both parents must be such that in their children's eyes they seem truly one, a seamless unity. What the father has just solemnly refused in public cannot possibly be obtained from the mother in some roundabout way, and vice-versa. This parental harmony is obviously the indispensable condition for a healthy influence on the children. At the same time, it is an admirable image of God who is both tender and strong at the same time.

Between the spiritual accompanist and his partner, or between a religious superior and his brothers, things are a little less simple. In principle, the one is alone and, by this very fact, much more helpless. When it is appropriate that he show himself firm and strong, his strength risks hardening him and making him appear oppressive and unjust. On the other hand, when he thinks he must show himself kind and understanding, his goodness risks overwhelming him and making him seem too easy-going. The Whip-Them-Into-Shape- Father-Superior and the Sugar-Coated-Daddy-Superior are not purely imaginary figures. And even if these nicknames are unjust because they do not necessarily correspond to the objective reality of the leader in question, they do nonetheless express a subjective reality lived by those who use the nicknames to protect themselves against a type of intervention which they experience, rightly or wrongly, as frustrating or wounding.

Harmonizing strength and tenderness surely constitutes one of the most difficult goals to attain and most delicate to maintain at the heart of spiritual accompaniment. As it is the image of God which is here in play in each one of us, we will understand that as perfect a solution as humanly possible is given us only in holiness, which is never complete here below. Only the charity of a saint, identified with the Holy Spirit in that saint, can come close to having this harmony of the double image realized in him— and it is always a genuine miracle. Yet, lacking holiness and while humbly waiting for something better, we can find real help avoiding certain traps by being aware of the complementary demands of this divine love and of our personal greater or lesser possibilities or impossibilities in this respect.

These pitfalls are inherent in the transfer in every dialogue and in the unconscious scenario which each of the two partners plays out in this setting—of this we have already written at length. It is therefore important for the accompanist to know himself well enough, and to some extent to be aware of his possibilities, but especially of his limits in this regard. Better able to measure these limits, he will agree more readily to call on another person who may be able to play the complementary role—a brother who assists and supervises him or another leader in the community, or a confidant of the person accompanied, or even the community itself.

The first question he must ask himself has to do with which role he feels most at ease in: is it that of father or that of mother? To such a question, the answer should not be spontaneous; it must mature over time because it requires tactful discernment. In fact, it is not at all certain that the role in which one feels most at ease will also necessarily be the one most profitable for the partner in the dialogue. The contrary is sometimes true: what we believe to be our personal gift in this area also risks becoming a particularly weak key point.

Some people may perhaps think that the role we play most successfully necessarily goes along with our sex . A man would more easily be father; a woman would feel at ease as mother. Nothing is less certain, for several reasons. The first is found in the inevitable ambiguity reflected even in the physiology which goes along with being a sexual being. Each human being bears within both sides of the divine image. One of the two is very visible, but everyone has kept traces of the other. This is already true on the biological level, in the bodies of men and women, and even more evident, and with more consequences, on the psychological level. In his psychological makeup each human being possesses both masculine and feminine sides; between these, during his evolution, a certain selection has been made. At the end of this process, which may take years and is sometimes blocked along the way, one of the two sides is solidly and peacefully displayed at the front of his psychology and holds the place of an identity card. Usually this is the side corresponding to the person's biological gender. The other side has been interiorized, becoming a more underground identity which is always actively present and continues to exert an important and beneficial influence. A correctly interiorized feminine side prevents a man from becoming a monster of aggressivity and allows him also to recognize the woman outside himself when the time is right, and to orient his desire towards her. The same is true for the woman, who has correctly interiorized her masculine side. Of course, the dosages of this balance are infinitely variable. Sometimes they are also fragile. They can always be questioned and improved by meeting new people.

In this area, we can also encounter greater or lesser imbalances, the social consequences of which are rarely catastrophic. To be prepared for drawbacks, generally it is enough for the subject to have a slight knowledge of his possibilities and limits. For example, some men are uneasy with their feminine side, and some women are similarly ill at ease with their masculine side. The first case will produce excessively male men–those we call 'macho'; the second produces the *'femme fatale'* type of women, whose only weapon or means of communication is their subtly exploited charm. Some women, because of circumstances in their life, have needed to develop what has been called a supplementary masculine side, to have a greater interior strength. Similarly some men, as a consequence of other needs, have developed a supplementary feminine side to appear more attractive and more effective. All this is not abnormal, and it is not necessary to wish to change these balances at any cost. The men and women in question would lose part of their natural attractiveness and part of their psychological identity. It is enough for them to learn to know themselves as they are and to accept themselves that way, knowing that the sum of the qualities they present in this area credits them with both strong points and weak points. No one is perfectly harmonious in this respect save God, who is perfectly father and perfectly mother. Generally, these inevitable limits do not imply any risk, but only particular possibilities: an opportunity which is important to recognize in order to manage it better.

As we are never alone in a relationship of accompaniment, our opportunities and our limitations are at the same time determined by the more or less conscious attitude of the person coming to us. Which side of the accompanist is this brother or sister addressing? The masculine or the feminine side, or both at the same time? The father or the mother or a subtle mixture of both? The answer to this question is not unimportant. This does not mean that the accompanist's attitude necessarily has to be perfectly in tune with the scenario unconsciously chosen by the partner. We have already said that the opposite will sometimes be more useful. If, for example, someone appeals strongly to the maternal side of his spiritual father—and there is no contradiction in this hypothesis—, this can come from the fact that as a young adult he was never able or never dared to confront his own father or any other father figure. He continues to flee the father and to seek refuge near a maternal figure. The best response to this expectation is probably not to set him—symbolically, of course—on the knee of a new mother, but no doubt, on the contrary, gently to evade the role he would like to impose on his guide; in this way, he will eventually be able to measure himself against, and if necessary bump into, a normally strong father image, this time an image which is less conflicted and more easily assimilated and which can in the end render pointless this attempt at endlessly replaying past frustrations. Of course, in a case like this, if the accompanist agreed to replay the mother's role, the person accompanied could draw an immediate benefit from this, as sometimes would the accompanist as well if this role corresponded to his own inner bent. But the long-term result, especially if this game prolongs itself to the point of closing in upon itself, would be practically nil.

It is not always easy to discern clearly which of the two

roles, the father's or the mother's, is called for by the partner. By this we mean not an explicit, but an implicit, because largely unconscious, request. This is sometimes expressed in so disguised a way that one can easily be mistaken about the true impact of the request. This risk is even more real because everyone will always tend to interpret the signals of the request through the prism of his own scenario and thus his own unconscious needs. The accompanist might, for example, have the impression that the other person needs a warm, comprehensive welcome when in fact it is urgent he be shown some fatherly firmness. The error in this analysis can easily be explained if, for example, the accompanist, without realizing it, were preoccupied with sparing others the affective frustrations which he himself suffered from his own mother, sufferings, intolerable at the time, which were repressed and buried in his unconscious for a long time.

Since Freud, we all know that the weight of the paternal and maternal symbolism is linked with what he called the Oedipus Complex and with its more or less happy resolution. Fusional communion with the mother before birth and during the first few years after birth was threatened by the father, who was also linked to the mother by a totally different and completely distinct affective bond from which the child feels forever excluded. Thenceforth he holds an image of the mother as an object ardently desired and irrevocably lost. The father's image, on the other hand, will call upon the original taboo which separates the child forever from the object of his desires. If this process occurs in an affective climate where the mother is sufficiently warm and reassuring and the father shows all the necessary firmness, the child will agree to pass from his dream world to the real world without any inhibiting trauma, definitively leaving the mother's womb to confront exterior reality. He will be able to interiorize the object of his desire which, even when absent, will be present affectively in his inner world, and by this fact he will create a space where, little by little, he can develop his autonomy and his freedom and try out his capacity for loving other beings different from the one he totally identified with during the first stage of his life. Even if this process occurs in a relatively satisfactory way at the appropriate time, which is not always the case, it is never completely finished. Each new meeting, especially those where love in all its various forms comes into play, should allow a person to begin the more or less frustrating, more or less liberating scenario again, and refine its fragile success more and more.

Without his being aware of it, obviously, such memories, with all their inevitable existential baggage, will color the accompanist's bond with those who look for a father or a mother in him, or towards whom he feels called to play one of these roles. In this sense it may be of use to become well aware of which values are specifically paternal, that is, what impact a child expects from his father, and which are the specifically maternal values or the impact he expects from his mother in the oedipal process as it evolves in as satisfactory a way as possible (that is to say, never fully).

The mother excels in lovingly welcoming; she listens, understands before things are said, she restrains herself from intervening, she is patient, tolerant, she lets be and lets do, she consoles, she enfolds with affection. At one point in our evolution, such a presence is absolutely vital and indispensable. But by itself it is not enough. Without the paternal intervention which marks the start of a separation between the child and the mother, it would produce only persons without backbone, unable to confront the harsh realities of life.

By coming between the mother and the child, the father's image will always remain marked by the painful and incomprehensible frustration of what is forbidden. But by opening a space where the child can learn to exercise his autonomy and freedom, the father is also the one who calls him by name, reveals his identity to him, opens a path, gives him a task, confirms his first successes, and invites him to identify with himself and go further than he did. The father is a source of strength and solidity which the child will test by confronting him, for we do not fall asleep in our father's arms; on the contrary, we walk with him, measure ourselves against him, confront him and struggle with him, we try to imitate him, do as he does and do even better. There is nothing more thrilling or affectively more positive for a child between the ages of six and ten than games with his father at which he tries to win, and at which the father from time to time lets him have the surprise and pride of winning. But this confrontation and rivalry are truly fruitful only to the degree that they take place within the warm affective climate fostered by the mother, and with the child experiencing the perfect communion between father and mother.

The complementary presence of the father and the mother is indispensable to the education of young children, because in these circumstances no one alone can assume both facets of the parental role. Moveover, life itself holds a secret of parental stand-ins: grandparents, big brother, big sister, uncles, aunts, teachers, and so on, are so many substitute fathers and mothers. When it comes to spiritual teaching where an adult, or an adult in the making, is the object, the parental figures can be incarnated by the accompanist without eliminating recourse to a third person, as we have already said. There again, life itself knows how successfully to vary the dose appropriate to each scenario according to circumstances; an optimism which, it is understood, has value only within a freeing dialogue of accompaniment.

To be more precise, let us add that if there is in principle one accompanist, the simple presence of a third person—as it were behind the relationship—can be extremely precious, without any necessity of speaking of this as a true three-way relationship. This is relatively easy in a religious community where by force of circumstance, other persons besides the novice master are more or less close and play a significant role in the eyes of the person accompanied: a confessor, superior, professor, perhaps a confrère who is a friend. As long as there is perfect communion between the accompanist and this person, such a 'presence' has much to be said for it, because it can be a positive complementary influence.

The classic case comes in the sometimes excellent and sometimes difficult, but always delicate, collaboration between the novice master and the major superior, abbot, or provincial. This collaboration is all the more delicate in the benedictine family, where the novice master exercises his office—at least in theory—subordinate to the Father Abbot to whom Tradition confides a kind of global spiritual fatherhood over the whole life of the monastery, novices included. This vision of things no doubt conforms to Tradition and deserves respect. Psychologically, however, it is important that the novice master's role be fully promoted so that there can be no doubt in the novice's eyes about the dominant role that he exercises. Having two Fathers is not good, or even thinkable, for the novice. The abbot's role is not obscured or avoided for all that. In addition to his deep communion with the novice master, which must be obvious to everyone, by his simple presence the abbot will contribute positively to the novice's spiritual growth, without any need to says a lot of things or hold periodic interviews which might easily be a source of confusion to the novice.

A relationship of accompaniment will inevitably evolve as the person accompanied makes progress. It must not be frozen in certain rites or be held to timetables which tend with time to become immutable. It is appropriate to be particularly attentive to the subtle signs which the person being accompanied will make, unknowingly for the most part, to let it be known that new questions are arising and he is experiencing a need for a different type of relationship. At the beginning, the need to be listened to at length and the necessity of free expression have a legitimate priority over everything else. A bond, a reciprocal confidence, an intimacy are created which have a certain affective warmth. This is the first fruit of conversations responding to every person's need to feel he is understood and accepted without judgment, even taken in charge, through the accompanist's listening.

Yet this affective bond, so vital at this stage of accompaniment, can bear full fruit only if, at the next stage, a new disposition is manifested by the accompanist's attitude: a certain strength or firmness which will recall the father's role. Not only must the accompanist be able to listen to the other with respect and extreme attention, with a quality of love capable of accepting just as he reveals himself, but he must also be able to create some distance between the other and himself, a distance which will become a place of freedom for the other person. This is the secret of every true love. The accompaniment relationship must in no way cause two persons to regress towards some sort of fusional form similar to what existed before birth, or close them in on each other. Its aim is eventually to create a distance vitally impregnated with love. Only such a very clear distance, in a love just as clear and assured, can create the space two people absolutely need in order to take an important step in their personal evolution together, but each person for himself, and to exercise their freedom towards one another in total autonomy. Because at this depth in the relationship, both partners benefit equally from the accompaniment.

It is not always easy to sense the particular moment at which it is appropriate to let the relationship evolve. A change in the vocabulary or the feelings of the person accompanied, or an unspoken, but less and less well controlled, aggressiveness, for example, can be the sign. New needs come to light in the psychology of the person accompanied. This is simply proof that the listening and welcome freely bestowed during the first stage are beginning to bear fruit. The accompanist is not always ready to interpret these signs correctly. He may hesitate to change a strategy which has succeeded very well thus far. All the more if, unaware enough of the subtle play of transfer and counter-transfer, this first strategy happened to be in full harmony with his own scenario and, by that fact, with his own unconscious needs. The affective commitment of both parties in the relationship receives its full meaning only if it implies that the accompanist is prepared to evolve with the other person and the new needs which progressively come to light in him. In most cases, this means going from a rather maternal attitude to one more explicitly paternal.

These explanations and warnings are clear only on paper. In fact, not everyone is equally gifted for both roles at once. On the other hand, especially, it is not obvious that such a change is possible for most accompanists, given the psychological and affective capital invested in one specific form during the first stage. The difficulty comes not only from the accompanist. The fragility of the person accompanied is also involved. Too brutal a change of strategy by the former might completely disorient the latter and make him regress towards earlier stages, and this might translate itself concretely into depression in various forms. Everything depends on the case, obviously, and on the depth of certain old wounds whose pain or anguish still secretly lurk in him. Then one must know how to act with great tact and prudence, temporarily delaying the distancing to wait for a more opportune moment, sometimes knowing how to yield a little, all the while knowing that one day, with the help of events or encounters, the distance must unfailingly be created, simply because it is the indispensable condition for freedom for both of them.

Acting with prudence will often mean becoming attentive to the other person's reactions. When the accompanist tries to create distance, the subject will in return give him all kinds of signals that he will have to be able to interpret at their true value. For example, the person accompanied will try to mobilize his attention again, when his real interest would be to embrace the distance, to try to walk at his own pace and rhythm. As always, the important thing is to link the distancing and the permanence by the bond of love. The distance created must never give the subject the impression of being once again the victim of rejection. All appearance of rejection, or what may be experienced by the subject as rejection, without valid reason, could have only dire consequences and delay the maturing process once again. The person accompanied must concretely experience the degree to which love remains and the bond always persists, even while it is deepening. It is thanks to the bond remaining and the distance being at the same time created that the person accompanied has some chance of being returned to his own autonomy and responsibility and thus maturing towards truly adult behavior.

Life lived in common by most religious, with all its unavoidable restraints, is an important element which can play a regulating role in the creation of the right distance between the accompanist and the person accompanied. The larger the group or community, the greater the constraints will be. They can come into play at any level, and depend first of all on the time available for each person. If a novice master is lucky enough to have six novices in the novitiate, each novice theoretically has a right to one-sixth of the novice master's available time. That one of the brothers should, for example, habitually occupy half his time is completely unthinkable. The constraint imposed by the lifestyle is by that very fact purely external to the relationship and thus all the more precious. If this principle of reality is ordinarily respected, it can show itself to be very fruitful. If it is not, the bond between the two will have trouble bearing fruit within the group. Both the accompanist and the one accompanied are part of the group dynamic and the latter's attainment of maturity necessarily implies a minimum of respect for this dynamic.

One last word about the difficulties which can arise when the person accompanied presents serious gaps in the integration of the image of father or mother which color his current behavior. Either he has not known one or both of his parents (even though acceptable substitutes may have compensated for such an absence during his childhood), or one or both parents, although physically present, demonstrated serious deficiencies in exercising the parental role. Cases can vary infinitely, and each should be evaluated by itself, taking into account each person's personal history. One cannot make a general rule. Some significant examples can suggest the spirit in which such deficiencies should be managed.

When the mother, for example, has been notoriously deficient, or even totally absent, it may be impossible for the child to feel love or recognize love from another person. This kind of fundamental insensitivity is first manifest in relationships with persons, but we can often find it in the relationship with God and even in the prayer life. The subject experiences a sort of total reticence, a real allergy towards everything which might allow him to experience God sensibly as warmth, tenderness, consolation. It is a kind of paralysis of feelings which predisposes him to chronic aridity in the life of prayer. The patient and prolonged sharing of these feelings—or rather these non-feelings—with an informed accompanist can sometimes allow awareness of the wound at the origin of such a block to surface. Otherwise, this block will lead to a systematic refusal to experience love—an unconscious refusal, of course, for which the subject bears no responsibility.

In other cases, perhaps more frequent today, the maternal role dominated, sometimes even exclusively. Many young people have been spoiled by attention and love to the point of making the father image fade or disappear almost completely. They generally present contradictory symptoms. They are at one and the same time fascinated by love, which they keep demanding at every meeting that comes along, and horrified at that same love. Despite their need for love, they experience any love shown them as a form of oppression and bullying which stifles them psychologically. This is not immediately apparent to someone who observes them superficially. They seem to be looking for a maternal figure to give them security and peace. Much more deeply, however, they are calling out to a father without knowing it, a father who would be able to disengage them from too demanding and invasive a maternal image. It often follows that any gesture or expressed sense of love will remind them of the mother who became overpowering or, worse still, the mother who, without realizing it, played the father's role.

In fact, it is not so much the mother's role which was deficient in most cases today, but rather the father's role. Since the european student strikes in May 1968, when it was 'forbidden to forbid', most fathers—and this is true even in religious life—seem to have become rather ashamed or even feel guilty about the role which normally devolves on them. Of course there has always been an oppressive way of being a father and that has become unacceptable today. But for a young person to acquire his full autonomy, an expression of real firmness remains an absolute necessity, which is impossible without a minimum number of 'don'ts'. Some fathers have tried to avoid a firmness considered excessive by trying to play the mother's role, with consequences just as harmful and, in addition, the risk of confusion between the two roles and an affective blackmail that can lead to the profit or detriment of authority and power. This blackmail can sometimes be found in the religious community and can go both ways, under such rather subtle forms as: 'If you do not obey, it is because you do not love me', or 'If you do not obey, I will no longer love you'; or, the other way round: 'If you love me, you owe me this permission'.

The repercussions of this lack of the father, or the confusion of his role with the mother's, are easy to detect in young people. They show, to some degree, an acute lack of a sense of identity. Many young people lack confidence, doubt themselves, do not know who they are or what they should be. They lack confidence in their own potential and are afraid to commit themselves. They seem changeable and fickle. They seem to lack backbone and their life lacks stability and guidelines. In popular language, we call such a child 'spoiled', just as we speak of a fruit being spoiled by having been exposed too long to the warmth of the sun; here it is to the intimate and fusional warmth of the maternal influence.

On the other hand, the father's role may have been dominant in the subject's life, overdeveloped to the point of being experienced as truly oppressive and paralyzing. It is only normal that the wounds inflicted then have a tendency to reopen every time an authority figure looms on the horizon. These subjects can be seriously allergic to any form of authority, excessively critical and aggressive. Their relationship with the leader will tend to deteriorate very quickly to the level of arm wrestling or permanent conflict. Here again, only coming to an awareness of the wound which underlies such a hardening, an awareness which can only be the fruit of a long journey of listening and exchange, can at length resolve a conflict for which neither of the partners is really responsible.

Spiritual accompaniment must take such situations into account, without necessarily pretending to resolve them all. In many cases, this would need an investment of time and a professional competence beyond that of a simple novice master or confessor. Yet by simply being who he is, by patiently listening to the endlessly repeated story of the brother or sister in question, the accompanist can considerably improve the situation without even being aware of doing so, without any claim other than love. The simple quality of the bond between him and the brother, welded in listening to him and to what God wants to say through the secrets he confides, can at length bear surprising fruits, even in the psychological realm. We have seen that God is not outside psychology; he is at work in and through the subject's psychological makeup. Every psychological development has a meaning and an orientation which are no stranger to God's creative movement. To the extent that, within the relationship, without falling too quickly into a falsely 'supernatural' way of speaking, the accompanist can remain attentive to this creative and liberating movement—that is, the Spirit of God who is moving somewhere within this psychology—extraordinary upheavals can occur which look like a true rebirth of the person. It is as if a new person were being born from the relationship of accompaniment and from that love which, at the heart of the relationship and in a thousand ways, every spiritual guide tries to radiate in the name of the Lord Jesus and in the strength of his Spirit.

DISCERNING
the WILL of GOD 9

God's Will and 'self will'

IN THE PRECEDING PAGES, we have
repeated over and over that all spiritual accompaniment should lead to putting us back in touch with our
deepest reality, our life at its source in the innermost depth
of our heart. This is not an easy task, because we habitually live at the surface of our being, and we have generally
lost contact with this deepest core. What is more, the ac-
cesses to it are generally no longer available or are very
obstructed. How can we patiently, throughout our life,
clear this way to make it accessible again? How can we
patiently let this current, which carries us along interiorly, unfortunately without our knowing it, come to the
surface of our consciousness?

The intuition of this deep life, translated by modern psychology into terms such as 'unconscious' and 'poles of
identity', is not strictly the domain of psychology. Basing
its discussions on and supporting some of its theories by
this intuition, psychology concurs with a very old observation which was already at work in the words and counsel of spiritual writers at the beginning of monasticism.
Only their vocabulary is different from ours. We could
quote more specifically Origen or Evagrius, whose experience was transmitted to us in the West by John Cassian
and who are at the starting point of a rich spiritual tradition with its own particular and already very precise vocabulary. By oversimplifying, we could sum up what some
might call their 'spiritual psychology' as follows: At the
deepest part of every human person is the *noûs*. This is not
limited to 'intelligence' or 'reason' to the extent that these

words refer to the faculty of thinking and reasoning. Much more deeply, the *noûs* is identified with the deep heart, the spirit (*mens* in Latin). For the ancients, the *noûs* is the place of God within us *(ho topos tou Theou)*, the place where God dwells in us and from which he sends us his impetus and allows us to participate in his life increasingly more and more. It is there, too, in the *noûs* of every human being, that we can find God's absolutely unique plan for that person. By all the evidence, this plan is a plan of love, and it can only correspond to the greatest possible flowering of the full capacity of being and developing that each person possesses.

This plan of love coincides with the desire God has for each one of us. It is because God loves a person that God desires him to be this or that—that is, unique. There is nothing arbitrary in such a disposition, except the arbitrariness of love which can but fulfill beyond all expectation. This desire of God is equal to his 'will' according to the first etymological meaning of the greek word *thelèma*. God's will for human beings is what God wants for them and it is the fruit of his love. It is in fact practically synonymous with love. Manifestly, nothing more perfect, more agreeable, more profoundly joyous could ever happen to a human being outside this desire or this will of God for him.

Unfortunately, it is not easy for people to reach this will of God within them. As a consequence of the first fall, this desire of God—the source of each person's interior unity, from which he could have gone peacefully and without conflict towards complete fulfillment without even going through trial and death—has been obscured in him. His interior unity has been wounded and checked. It burst and was scattered in a multitude of little fragmented and superficial desires which take centre front in him, pull him in every direction and prevent him from becoming aware of God's true desire within him. According to a somewhat simplistic but eloquent schema, the ancient authors picture the multiplicity of desires or self-wills as being crystallized around man's deep heart in a kind of opaque envelope which obscures God's desire and prevents it from taking over that person and being radiated from his centre. Another image would be that of a screen set up between the superficial self and the deep self. Self-wills are a hindrance to the deep heart's listening and take man far away from the ways of interiority. The deep desire is then like water which loses itself in sand: it can neither spring up nor be reached.

In the depths of each human person, the place of God in us, reigns an absolute *katastasis,* to use Evagrius' vocabulary. The best translation of this greek term seems to be 'repose'. God in person is this 'repose' and creates within a human person this tranquil stability, in contrast to the extreme mobility of his superficial desires or self-will. In the writings of Evagrius, the term *katastasis* is practically synonymous with prayer. More exactly, it designates a 'state of prayer': it is there, in fact, that prayer dwells in each baptized person. Prayer is at work, untiringly, once someone has received the grace of baptism. Alas! once again the desires or wills or thoughts *(logismoi)* surround the human heart and prevent it from attaining this interior repose at the deepest part of the self, where the Spirit's prayer is constantly at work, where God's will is also found, that is, as we have just said, his deepest and most authentic desire.

It seems important to underline this way of conceiving things, quite common in ancient literature. Indeed, in modern times, a certain spiritual literature has insisted on the crucifying character of God's will. Do we not say that it is important to renounce self-will to go along with God's will? This might give us the impression that God's will must be something painful, something, as it were, suspended above our head like a sword of Damocles, whose painful edge we will feel sooner or later. Reality, thankfully, does not conform completely to this image. Although it is undeniable that the fulfillment of God's will for us sometimes entails real sacrifices, still at its deepest level, it can only coincide with our most harmonious development and perfect happiness. Similarly, our complete development can only coincide with the will of God for us.

Ancient monastic literature also insists very much on renouncing self-will, but we must understand this in the light of the concept just presented. Over the centuries the term 'will' has undergone a considerable change in meaning. In thomistic tradition, for example, and in modern philosophy in general, the term 'will' designates the faculty of love, the source of freedom. It is obvious that there can never be a question of renouncing this will. On the contrary, it is important to free this deep will in human beings, to the degree that it is still temporarily subjected to numerous superficial desires where the heart is divided.

Now, one of the most effective ways of liberating this profound will is precisely by renouncing self-will. This is obedience in the sense the ancients understood it. When they speak of obedience, they do not mean in the first place obedience to a leader as it is practiced in any group or community, whether political or religious. Instead, they consider obedience a true spiritual therapy, an event which involves the whole human person, thanks to which he is deeply transformed, his profound being is freed and lets him know his hidden desire. To put it as simply as possible: in the human being who has totally renounced his scattered self-will, only the will of God—that is to say, God's plan of love for him—remains and becomes recognizable in him.

One of the earliest desert sayings will serve to illustrate this 'therapy-by-obedience'. We owe it to Abba Poemen:

> Abba Poemen said, 'The will of man is a brass wall between him and God and a stone of stumbling. When a man renounces it, he is also saying to himself, "By my God,

I can leap over the wall". *(Ps 17:30 [Hebr. 18:29])*. If a man's will is in line with what is right, then he can really labour. On the contrary, if he tries to justify and maintain his will, he runs a great danger.'[1]

The meaning of this saying is clear enough: because self-will is like a wall between God and man, between the deep self and the superficial self, it is advisable to break down this wall, which is an obstacle, in order to be able to reestablish contact with God. Put more clearly: the only really necessary thing to do is to renounce self-will. Deeper than any self-will is the will of God, which each person possesses within, the only will that matters in leading him to his full development.

From this comes the somewhat incisive—not to say cruel—terminology which ancient monastic literature commonly uses to describe this surgery of the self-will: it speaks of 'renouncing', 'cutting off' *(koptein)*, even of 'hating'.[2] This vocabulary has no lack of harshness and it is good to un-dramatize it. There is, in fact, a way of fighting against self-will which gives it too much importance and risks producing the opposite effect. On the contrary, most often one need only stop being preoccupied with them, nothing more; not holding on to them and, simply by doing this, silencing them. Above all, it is important ceaselessly to prefer the deeper desires as soon as they make themselves felt in the very depth of our heart, beyond the silence of our superficial desires.

In the seventeenth century, in the wake of the ignatian tradition, the term 'indifference' was used to designate this interior disposition. It is important to understand this term correctly. It never means becoming insensitive to desires–this would be to fall into a supreme illusion, with

---

1. *The Sayings of the Desert Fathers,* Poemen, 54 [CS 59:174]. The final sentence is translated from *Apophtegmes.*
2. *RB* 4.60 : *voluntates proprias odisse.*

all the risks of psychological unbalance foreseeable in such a circumstance—but to put one's own preferences in brackets in order to be available to follow God's desire-will as soon as the divine preference makes itself felt some way or another. Curiously, as early as the twelfth century, in a sermon about the discernment of spirits, Saint Bernard had already given a perfect description of this indifference, which one might think had come from the pen of Saint Ignatius himself. Of course, Bernard thinks, some desires are evidently in conformity with God's will, and others are just as clearly contrary to it. But there are really doubtful cases in which it would not be advisable to make a hasty decision and in which it is important to know how to watch for an interior sign of grace:

> There are cases [writes the abbot of Clairvaux] about which we can know nothing for certain and where our will can decide nothing with certitude. Let it then remain suspended between the two solutions, without attaching itself too much to one or the other, remembering constantly that the other choice might please God more. Let us thus remain ready to follow his will, as soon as we know that it inclines towards either side[3].

This suspension, this 'indifference' or disposition to silence one's superficial desires and attach no decisive importance to them while waiting for a sign from God, will evidently play an important role in spiritual discernment as it is practiced in accompaniment. Indifference facilitates access to God's desire, and at the same time making the choice of God's will in preference to any other desire. A concrete example, better than extended reflection, will

3. *Sermo de diversis*, 26:3.

allow us to understand how renouncing desires frees in each person a still deeper desire, which is that of God.

The example is taken from a story the late Father Jean-Claude Guy sj cast in the form of a parable in which he gathered some stray bits of information from the writings of Saint Ignatius and accounts about him. The parable was designed to illustrate the way the saint practiced spiritual discernment when he handed out obediences. The scene takes place in Rome, towards the end of Ignatius' life. The Society by that time was well-established in the Italian peninsula, where it has opened much appreciated colleges in large cities. One day, two college teaching positions needed to be filled: one in Naples and the other in Venice. At that moment, Ignatius had only one available candidate. He had to choose one of the two colleges and temporarily sacrifice the other. Now, the Society's situation in these two cities was very different. In Venice, the Fathers were venerated by everyone and enjoyed the authorities' complete trust. When they crossed the streets, people pressed around them to ask their blessing and kiss their footsteps. In Naples, it was just the opposite. The Society was scorned by almost everybody and the civil authorities suspected it of grim machinations. The Fathers hardly dared go out into the street for fear of the stones being thrown at them by urchins. How to choose between the two colleges for the only available candidate? How to determine where the will of God for him lay?

But before continuing this story, let us imagine for an instant not Saint Ignatius but some other person—say, a contemporary superior—in this situation. By what criteria could he act as a wise superior? Perhaps he could try to reflect on the human and spiritual qualities of the sole candidate, to see which of the two situations would be more appropriate for him. Is he solid in his vocation? generous enough? not too impressionable or depressive? somewhat energetic and aggressive? If yes, perhaps one could run the risk of exposing him to the neapolitan situ-

ation. If not, would it not be more prudent to send him to
Venice and wait for a more seasoned candidate to face
Naples? Such reasoning is correct and indicates real pru-
dence. This would certainly not be a bad way to proceed.

This is not, however, how Ignatius acted because he
was convinced that the candidate bears the answer in his
own heart and that it is not for the superior, or even for
the general superior, to make this discernment for him.
He sent for him, laid the problem out to him, describing
as accurately as possible the two very different situations
in Venice and Naples.

We may pose yet another question before continuing
the story: what would any other candidate have done when
Saint Ignatius explained the predicament? Some—perhaps
even most, perhaps even all—moved by spontaneous generosity, would spontaneously have opted for Naples, where
the Society was in a fine mess. Is it not appropriate to
always prefer the more difficult and contrary situation?

Saint Ignatius did not even give the candidate time to
choose this way—that is, to choose by his spontaneous
generosity—because although in his eyes that would be a
generous and meritorious choice, it would nevertheless
be a bad spiritual discernment. It is not at all certain, in
fact, that the most contrary thing corresponds always and
everywhere to God's desire and concrete will for someone. An *a priori* 'it is preferable to choose the most contrary thing' offers no guarantee that this comes from the
Holy Spirit. It even has a great chance of expressing one
of the innumerable self-wills very common to every human being. Is there not such a thing as a tense will, making 'always and everywhere the most perfect' choice—
which is perhaps the most treacherous self-will of all?
Recalling here what has previously been said about some
interior authorities unique to each person, we may even
be permitted to think that such an apparently virtuous *a
priori* is almost certainly dictated by that someone now very
familiar to the reader, the interior policeman. And by him

alone. There he is, caught red-handed, without any link to the Holy Spirit and God's desire.

What did Ignatius do then, fully conscious of the intrinsic ambiguity of any answer which is too immediately generous? After having described the respective situations in Venice and Naples, he sent the candidate to the chapel to pray for three hours, asking him only one thing: that he renounce as perfectly as possible his personal preferences regarding the two proposed solutions, whatever the good intentions or the objections which went along with them. In other words—those of Saint Ignatius—the candidate must establish himself in a 'holy indifference' towards them, remaining equally open to both solutions. Then, when the three hours of prayer are finished, come back to him. The candidate did this, and three hours later returned to Ignatius, who asked him: 'Do you think that you have now renounced your own will about this?' The young Jesuit answered: 'To the degree that I am able to know it, yes, Father, I think I have renounced my own will.' At this, Ignatius continued: 'So, now, what do you really want?' And Ignatius' secretary added this comment: 'Because Ignatius knew that, in someone who has completely renounced his own will, the desire that then remains in his heart coincides exactly with the will of God for him.'[4]

We could not find a better illustration of what we may call the 'therapeutic' character of obedience, inasmuch as

---

4. Father Guy was inspired by several texts published by Gonçalves de Camara, in his *Mémorial* (translated into French by R. Tandonnet, *Christus* collection, 20, Paris, 1966), numbers 114, 116, 117, 263, 337. Father Aimé Solignac, to whom we owe this information, comments on the story imagined by his confrère: 'The method is . . . purely ignatian. Ignatius asked above all, for himself and his sons, to *"feel* the will of God and to *accomplish* it perfectly". Now, both verbs presuppose a total abnegation of self-will (Ignatius insisted on this more than on prayer) and attentiveness to the movements and "anointing" of the Holy Spirit. All in all, he desired his commandment to reach the "interior commandment" given each person by the Spirit' (Letter to the author dated 27 February 1992).

this is a renouncing of self-will for the purpose of allowing God's will to be revealed and felt in someone. As long as someone has really renounced every superficial desire which prevents him from reaching his deep self where God is at work, he can always rely on the desire which remains quietly at the deepest place within him. This desire, there is no possible doubt, is God's desire for him. Because obeying God is always obeying the deepest urge within us to what is best and truest in every human being.

Considering obedience and renunciation of self-will in this way is not to undervalue how painful and trying they often are. Here below, obedience will never be 'painless'. Most of the time, reaching one's deepest self through obedience will be experienced as a real death. But if we die to our superficial self, we do so to be born to our true self. If we die to our superficial desires, we do so to be born to God's desire in our regard. This is the only condition of real growth.

DISCERNING OUR PERSONAL MEASURE

God's will for human beings is concretized by the measure of grace placed at our disposal to be put into practice. When God asks something, he gives everything needed to bring his design to a successful conclusion: health, ability, time, and also that inward impulse which theology calls grace and which humans constantly need to act in conformity with the will of God. There can be no doubt about this, because God cannot contradict himself. This simple observation about the obvious already reveals some criteria which allow the will of God to be discerned unfailingly. It is useless to strain one's health, to presume on one's strength or abilities, to transform one's life into a race against the clock. If we lack the health, the abilities, or simply the time to embark on what we believe to be

God's will, it is probable that illusion is very close. What is more difficult to discern—yet remains most important—is the grace that God places or does not place at one's disposal, and which does or does not urge someone from within, letting him know that this is or is not, in fact, his will.

The ancient authors, Eastern and Western, had a specific term for this impulse of grace implying a personal call from God. They called it 'measure'—in Greek *metron*, in Latin *mensura*. In the various areas of christian life, and most specifically where a portion is left to personal initiative, each believer has received his particular measure. The term is frequent in ancient monastic literature, and Saint Benedict, for example, still commonly used this vocabulary. He speaks of the measure of food and drink, a measure unique to each individual and one he refused to over-specify except to determine, in general, an honest average suitable for the whole community.[5] Why does Saint Benedict hesitate like this? Some might think that he was taking into account the diversity of health or generosity of each person. This is not the profound reason invoked by Saint Benedict. His motive was different: not all, he thought, have received the same measure of grace. In fact, Saint Benedict explicitly refers to the measure of each person's *ascesis as 'gift'*, this gift that all have received from God, quoting Saint Paul: 'Each one has received from God a particular gift: one of one kind and one of another'.[6] Thus, to determine the measure of *ascesis* for each person, it is of paramount importance to discern exactly the measure of the gift of grace each has received. Now, this does not necessarily coincide with the measure of health or the measure of generosity or each person's ability to endure privations. It is completely gratuitous. The measure of *ascesis* can only be made according to the measure of the grace a person receives very concretely from God in a particular situation.

This leads us to understand that this grace will always

5. *RB* 39 and 40.
6. *RB* 40.1, quoting *1 Cor* 7:7.

be strictly individual and thus legitimately different for different people. Grace can also evolve along with a person's christian experience. It should never be fixed once and for all. Instead, we should be wary of a tendency too quickly to codify certain ascetic habits which might end up becoming acquired reflexes devoid of spiritual impact. It is much more important in this regard to remain attentive to each new call from the Lord. Besides, the measure of grace and *ascesis* is usually lighter at the beginning and subsequently grows. But the opposite can also happen. What is important is not the quantity of the measure but, on the contrary, that at each instant in our evolution we be able to discern the portion of grace we have received so we can accord with it, without deviating in one direction or the other. For it would be just as harmful to go beyond the grace given than to fall short of it.

To describe the initiative of going beyond grace, ancient monastic literature invented the words *praesumere* and *praesumptio*. *Prae-sumere* means literally 'to seize too quickly, get hold of before the right time'. Our word 'presumption', which now has moral overtones it did not have earlier, comes from this same root. In its first meaning, the word simply meant: 'to want to appropriate for oneself a reality to which one is not yet called'. What it means it expresses well. When it comes to *ascesis,* the monk therefore presumes, not on his own strength, but on grace which is not yet given. Even if physical strength were enough to accomplish the work presumed, the spiritual benefit would be nil. Saint Benedict is absolutely categorical on this point: what is done without the spiritual father's blessing will be credited to presumption and vainglory, and not rewarded—*praesumptioni deputabitur ac vanae gloriae, non mercedi.*[7]

The desert Fathers had an extremely acute sensitivity to the illusions which could hide behind an ascetic life prac-

7. *RB* 49.9.

ticed outside any spiritual discernment. A wonderful saying of Poemen sums up this wisdom in a concise and striking sentence consisting in the original Greek of only six small words—and no less vigorous in english translation: "Anything without measure *(ametron)* comes from the devil'.[8] Anything outside the measure of the grace given, in fact or going beyond it, is surely an illusion coming from the evil one.

Another saying, attributed to an *Amma*—a spiritual mother—named Syncletica, is still more explicit:

> There is an *ascesis* which is determined by the enemy, and his disciples practice it. So how are we to distinguish between the divine and royal *ascesis* [which comes from God] and the demonic tyranny? Clearly through its symmetry *(symmetria)*, its quality of measure ... Indeed, lack of measure *(ametria)* always corrupts.[9]

The symmetry here consists precisely in the harmony between the measure of the grace given and what the ascetic wishes to accomplish. Whenever this measure is exceeded and someone lapses into *ametria*–and Syncletica's saying gives a lamentable example of this, fasting four or five days in a row to end up the following day in a pantagruelian feast—the ascetic is certainly the devil's plaything.

In spiritual accompaniment, this individual 'measure' of grace is even to be preferred to great spiritual principles, however excellent these may be in themselves, because they are sometimes inapplicable the way they are, simply because in this concrete case the measure of the grace received is different. Here is another example from

8. *Panta ta ametra ek tou diabolou, The Sayings of the Desert Fathers,* Poemen, 129. [CS 59:185]
9. *The Sayings of the Desert Fathers,* Syncletica, 15. [CS 59:233]

ancient monasticism. In the fourth and fifth centuries, one of the most controversial questions among monks was the appropriateness of manual labor: was it appropriate for a solitary, yes or no? Some monks, called messalians or euchites, were of the opinion that purely contemplative life not only allowed but required a rigorous abstention from any manual work, which could only distract them from continual prayer. This extreme position was quite quickly abandoned by most in favor of a 'middle' position: the monk could do manual work, but in his cell, without leaving it. Work in the fields outside his cell was forbidden. This, for example, is the position Saint John Cassian defended, contrary to Saint Benedict who allowed work outside in cases of necessity.[10] Traces of this controversy are present everywhere in ancient monastic literature, most particularly in the form of a theme which crops up from time to time, the theme of the 'little garden'. Does a monk have the right to cultivate vegetables in his garden? Saint Athanasius, in his *Life of Saint Anthony* answers affirmatively.[11] But a good number of sayings suggest a different teaching, which was no doubt more widespread and which Cassian reflects: it is not fitting for a monk to let himself be led into cultivating a little garden, a source of distraction. This is the principle which appeared sacrosanct no doubt in the eyes of many. Yet some of the sayings, while admitting the principle, in practice allow exceptions which each time are the fruit of a very thorough discernment.

As an example, this is an especially juicy anecdote, once again attributed to the great Poemen:

> A brother came to see Abba Poemen and said to him: 'I sow my field and give away in charity what I reap from it'. The old man said to him: 'That is good,' and the

10. *Conferences,* 24.4.
11. *Life of Saint Anthony,* 50.

brother departed with fervor and intensified his charity. Hearing this, Abba Anoub said to Abba Poemen: 'Do you not fear God, that you have spoken like this to the brother?' [So Anoub was an opponent of the 'little garden', and believed that Poemen shared the same principles]. The old man remained silent. Two days later, Abba Poemen saw the brother coming and in Abba Anoub's presence said to him: "What did you ask me the other day? I was not attending.' The brother said: 'I said that I sow my field and give away what I gain in charity'. Abba Poemen said to him: 'I thought you were speaking of your brother who lives in the world. If it is you [a monk] who are doing this, it is not right for a monk.' At these words, the brother was saddened and said: 'I do not know any other work, and I cannot help sowing the fields'. When he had gone away, Abba Anoub made a prostration and said: 'Forgive me'. Abba Poemen said: 'From the beginning, I too knew very well that sowing a field is not a monk's work, but I spoke to this brother as I did, adapting myself to his ideas and so I gave him courage to increase his charity. Now he has gone away full of grief, and yet he will go on as before, sowing his fields.'[12]

This is a good example of a discernment originally deficient but subsequently corrected. Poemen belonged to the school of those who considered outdoor work inappropriate for monks; he is, let us say, of the 'strict observance'.

12. *The Sayings of the Desert Fathers,* Poemen, 22 [CS 59:170].

Nevertheless, he listened attentively to the brother who put the question to him, and he quickly understood that the monk was not gifted at work indoors and that the out of doors was likely necessary for his balance. Above all, in this whole business, he recognized his deep desire, which was the desire to do charity. With what he earned with the vegetables from his garden, this brother was happy to give alms. A concession by Poemen, but bitter criticism from Abba Anoub who would have preferred to see the principle applied at once and in full rigor. To teach him a lesson, Poemen pretends to go back on his first discernment and reminds the brother of the principle in question. The brother is downcast, indeed discouraged and no doubt guilt-ridden, conscious of being a very poor monk. And all this to no purpose, because he was still led to cultivate vegetables again anyway! Unlike Anoub, Poemen was able to discern the true grace this monk had received, which was works of charity thanks to his work.

THE SIGNS OF GRACE

In this last saying, the mistaken discernment of Abba Anoub plunged a brother into sadness and discouragement. This is the *a contrario* sign that the directive was not in keeping with the Holy Spirit's urging. Indeed, Tradition is unanimous in recognizing by certain signs whether an envisaged path corresponds or does not correspond to the will of God or to an inner urging of the Holy Spirit. Certain spiritual authors have described and grouped these signs into a coherent system. Most of them may be boiled down to the sign Saint Benedict wants to see in the monk who would like to do additional penance during Lent. This can be fruitful only on two conditions: that the brother is able to do this 'in the joy of the Holy Spirit', and that he proceed 'with the abbot's consent and blessing'.[13] Both criteria are complementary. Without interior joy, any additional *ascesis* would only be 'constrained and forced'; without the discernment of an accompanist, any interior joy could become a source of illusion.

One of the earliest witnesses to an already solid teaching on the subject is a fifth-century byzantine bishop, Diadochus of Photicé. His writings, rediscovered in the West in the sixteenth century, greatly influenced the teaching of Saint Ignatius Loyola on the discernment of spirits. Diadochus develops a very specific teaching on the spiritual sensitivity suitable for discerning what is going on in our own heart and that of others. To designate this organ of discernment, he does not shy from using the greek term *aisthèsis,* translated 'sensitivity', 'sentiment'. Many people today would no doubt hesitate to use such an expression, because they are too used to being wary of their sentiments and to opposing feelings to faith. There is, however, a spiritual sensitivity which does not coincide entirely with superficial sensitivity—though it has some relationship to it—while already being an integral part of the experience of faith. In the tweflth century, Saint Bernard was also not shy of making abundant use of this sentimental or experiential vocabulary—in the best sense of the word: *sentire, consentire, praesentire, experiri, probare, frui,* etc. flow from his pen. This concerns a sentiment—both obscure and luminous— which enables us to have a premonition about certain things not sensed in the usual meaning of the word, yet which nevertheless provides an inner certainty that one is not mistaken. This is how Diadochus presents it:

> The sensitivity of the spirit *(noûs)* is an exact taste of the things we discern. As when we are not ill, our corporal sense of taste

13. *RB* 49.7-8.

discerns without error the good from the
bad in foods and we lean towards what is
sweet, so in the same way, when our spirit
begins to move in full health and great de-
tachment, it is able to sense divine consolation richly and not be drawn away by
what is opposed to it. As the body tasting
earthly sweetness is infallible in the experience of the sense, similarly when the spirit
rejoices over the tendencies of the flesh, it
can taste without error the Holy Spirit's
consolation: 'Taste', it is written in the
psalm, 'and see the sweetness of the Lord';
and by the action of charity it can retain an
unforgettable memory of that taste.'What
I ask in my prayer is that your charity grow
ever more and more in true knowledge and
in sensitivity *(aisthèsis)*, to discern what is
best'*(Ph 1:9-10)*.[14]

We should emphasize the second-last phrase: 'by the
action of charity it can retain an unforgettable memory of
that taste'. When a person is given the gift of sensing the
action of the Holy Spirit within, there remains an indel-
ible memory, a particular sensitivity inscribed on the
heart's memory, which becomes a reference point by
which he is able from then on to recognize the Holy Spirit's
action within himself or others, without delay and with a
minimum of risk of error.

To affirm this is also to underline the link between the
accompanist's personal spiritual experience and the help
he is called to give during dialogue with others. It is from
the starting point of remembering what has happened to
him in his relationship with the Lord that he can recognize the Lord's action in another person. As we pointed

14. Diadochus of Photicé, *Cent chapitres gnostiques*, 30.

out at the beginning of this book, there is no essential difference between recognizing the Spirit's touch through the Word of God at the time of *lectio*, for example, and discerning this same action in the desires or projects that another person comes to confide. In both cases, it is the same spiritual sensitivity, more or less refined by the memory of preceding experiences, which recognizes and correctly interprets the presence or absence of the Spirit.

This sensitivity to spiritual joy or the consolation received from God was admirably described and, so to speak, organized with a view to the practice of discernment by Ignatius of Loyola in the eight Rules of Discernment he left behind in his *Exercises*. There, Saint Ignatius starts from his experience during his long convalescence after the siege of Pamplona, during which he was intrigued by the alternation of consolation and desolation he seemed to notice in himself. He reveals himself at the same time heir to a long tradition of discernment in the Church, in particular the monastic tradition and he does not hesitate to call on it.

Already in the First Rule, he clearly distinguishes between what is proper to the action of God or his angels and what betrays the intervention of the evil spirit. The other Rules merely draw all the practical conclusions. It is therefore not without interest to quote the First here in its entirety:

> It is proper for God and his angels in their movements to give true happiness and spiritual joy, removing all the sadness and distress that the enemy inspires in us. It is proper to the latter to struggle against such rejoicing and spiritual consolation by proposing apparent reasons, subtleties and constant deception.

Among these consolations, Ignatius gives a special place

to consolations which come into the soul 'without prior cause' and which present themselves as sudden and inexplicable. These, he thinks, come infallibly from God, 'because it is characteristic of the Creator to enter, go out, move in the soul, pulling it completely into love of his divine majesty'. Since the impact of the evil one on the soul cannot go that deep, these motions can, without risk of error, be attributed to the action of the good spirit. But it is not the same for the motions which have a prior cause, even a good one—for example, a meeting, an exchange, a word of Scripture, a feeling of inner joy. Even if, at first, these impressions come from God, the evil spirit can seize them along the way to make them deviate from their path *(Rule Eight)*, because the evil one can also apparently confort the soul with the sole aim of dragging it down after himself. It is, moreover, characteristic of the evil one to present himself first as an angel of light, 'that is, he proposes good and wholesome thoughts in accordance with the just soul, and afterwards, little by little, he tries to bring it to himself by leading the soul in his hidden deceptions and perverse intentions' *(Rule Four)*. Thanks to God, the signs of such a perversion are clear enough: 'If the progression of our thoughts brings us finally to something evil or distracting or less good than what the soul first planned, or which weakens, worries and troubles the soul by removing the peace, tranquillity and repose it had before, it is a clear sign that it proceeds from the evil spirit' *(Rule Five)*. More detailed still is the description *Rule Seven* gives of the good and the evil angels' action:

> In those who are advancing from good to
> better, the good angel touches the soul gen-
> tly, lightly and sweetly, like a drop of water
> entering a sponge; the evil one touches
> sharply, with noise and agitation, like a drop
> of water falling on a rock . . . The cause is
> the soul's disposition . . . , when it is con-

trary to that of the angels, in fact, their entrance is noisy and perceptibly felt; when it is like they are, their entrance is silent as when a person goes through his own open door. *(Rule Seven).*

These few excerpts from Saint Ignatius are more than enough. Ignatius did not invent anything. Thanks to his particularly sharp perception of the psychology of man seeking the will of God, he was able to fine tune the traditional teaching on the criteria of spiritual discernment, which are consolation and joy.

A FEW PARTICULAR CASES

Before ending this chapter, we will mention a few more specific situations in which it is often very useful to be helped by an accompanist. There are three cases in which many believers—even those who have abandoned the practice of regular accompaniment—will spontaneously consult someone: choosing a state of life; difficulties in prayer; learning how to act with God. We need only apply concretely the process described in the preceding chapters.

THE CHOICE OF A STATE IN LIFE

In everyone's life, particularly crucial situations arise when one would like to be assured of having made a decision in full accord with God's will. It may be a possible vocation, for example, the choice of career or a companion for life. How is the accompanist to welcome a person who approaches him saying: 'I have an important decision to make, and I have come to ask your advice'?

The first certainty he must have is knowing that he does not possess the answer to the question just put to him.

Only the person asking has the answer within him. The counselor can only help him become aware of it. Of course, the basic question might be more or less hidden behind secondary questions, most of the time purely informative, which anyone could answer quite well. For example: to whom must one go to register at the seminary? What studies are necessary to be able to enter a monastery? The answers to such questions are at a level different than spiritual accompaniment. Once they have been given in the desired detail and the real question–what should I do?– imperceptibly comes up again, the dialogue's tone shifts and the two partners change their roles. From this moment, it becomes true once more that the accompanist no longer has a specific answer to give.

In fact, what is so marvelous about such a question is that the one asking holds the answer in the deepest part of his heart. The will of God he is seeking and sincerely wishing to embrace is nothing other than his deepest and most fruitful reality. As we have already said, the will of God does not threaten him in any way. It will not harm him in the least. It is nothing other than God's desire and love for him. There is nothing more fulfilling for him, in every sense of the word and according to every potentiality that God himself has placed in him.

The only difficulty lies in the fact that, until now, he has not been able to discern it clearly. And so he comes to ask a brother or a sister for help, but no one can ever help him unless they are aware that they know even less than he does. All they can do is listen respectfully and, by listening this way, teach him how to listen to his own heart and how to discern, little by little, there among a host of superficial desires and motivations, his deepest desire, the one which connects him to God. He must be able to let go and renounce all his little superficial urges, if need be, for the free will of God to spring up spontaneously in the deepest part of himself. Remember Saint Ignatius' question to his young Jesuit after three hours of prayer and 'holy indifference': 'Now, what do you really want?'

Basically, discerning God's will for someone should not be so difficult, since this has, so to speak, been entrusted to the accompanist in advance, in the very depths of his being, by the Holy Spirit who dwells in him from the moment of his baptism. It remains, however, not uncommon for the believer to be mistaken, sometimes even on important choices. Some choice which at the outset he sincerely believed to be God's will may at length be revealed to be an illusion. In his turn, he found himself caught in the murky and ambiguous world of his more or less skewed desires, which we call self-will. Thanks be to God, to err is never a catastrophe so long as we learn from it. It is precisely the experience of his own past errors that can help the accompanist correctly aid those who come to ask him for help. He can more easily prevent them in their turn from letting themselves be dazzled by what a hides God's desire for them from their eyes: their superficial wants, that bronze wall which Poemen reminded us above is the only obstacle and the only separation between the heart of man and his God.

Here again, we must listen attentively, without letting ourselves be put off by the various vague desires the speaker lets slip, which to the speaker's ears can easily appear to be whims. By being peacefully welcomed by someone they have the best chance of dissolving by themselves spontaneously in the heart of the person who opens himself up, leaving there there only this other sensitivity which will allow him to perceive within the depths of his being the desire of God, constitutive of his very being.

This may take some time. Again, we must avoid any hasty intervention which would stop the process of clarification and maturation which has begun through listening. Of course, it may happen that, right at the beginning of the conversation, aided by habit, the accompanist quite quickly perceives what the will of God may be in this specific case, or rather what it probably is not. Basic common sense or a few sufficiently obvious external signs can soon give even a slightly experienced observer no doubt on this, while the import of these same signs is still lost on the person doing the asking. Yet these reactions must not be manifested immediately, or suggested, or—still less—dictate to the other person's conscience, by saying, for instance: 'As for me, I think that . . . '; 'In my opinion, you must . . . '; 'No doubt God is asking you to . . . ' On the contrary, the other person must always be brought back to his own choice. Only he can make the decision in a truly fruitful way, that is, in full freedom. The accompanist can at the very most enlighten this choice with all the customary precautions, by prudently formulating a few questions, by suggesting a few complementary reflections to see how they touch the listener's heart—that is, how the Holy Spirit within him causes him to react. One may also, but with all the requisite tact, push aside the motivations which are manifestly not in conformity with the Gospel, or neutralize the desires to do good which under the guise of virtue are only the echo of injunctions from the super-ego or 'inner policeman'. But nothing more. What is important is not that the person obey his guide or even, we might say, that he take his advice into account. The important thing is that when the time comes—that is, when the movement of the Spirit becomes peacefully obvious in him—he be led to consent just as peacefully and sweetly, because God's will carries with it its own force of persuasion. It does not need exterior advice or comments. And the person who truly and clearly perceives God's will, or rather to whom it clearly manifests itself, immediately desires to obey it and is able joyfully to renounce everything contrary to it. This renunciation is, in fact, easy and hardly painful at all, because one is perfectly free and carried from within by this sweet and irresistible strength which springs up from himself.

A complication may arise because of the anguish which sometimes goes along with a preoccupation with being in accordance with God's will. Such anguish can cloud the issue and even paralyze a choice which should be spontaneous. It is always the sign that something else has stepped in the path of the person coming for consultation, something which emits false sounds which complicate the listening and discernment. The ideal would obviously be to discern the source and meaning of this false noise, so as to be able to treat it. In most cases, the accompanist does not have the time or the professional competence to do this. In other cases, in spite of attentive listening, it may be that no one desire clearly predominates and the subject remains torn between choices which seem to him equally desirable and valuable. This may be the sign that God simply is leaving the choice up to the person himself. And why not? The important thing sometimes–especially when there are such false noises–is not that one thing be chosen in preference to some other, but simply that he choose, and does so in complete freedom. In this case, the following speech may sometimes unblock the paralysis and lead to a perfectly valid choice: 'Here are all the arguments in favor of a positive choice. I believe you have perceived them well. And here on the other hand, are all the arguments in favor of a negative choice. You have perceived them equally well. If you choose the left, you choose well. If you choose the right, you choose equally well. The will of God for you, at this precise moment, is only that you truly choose something. Your choice will be God's will.'

DIFFICULTIES IN PRAYER

Here is another case where recourse to a spiritual accompanist is relatively frequent. Confidences such as 'I don't know how to pray any more', 'Prayer has become impossible' are in fact relatively frequent. Notice that the formulas used by the one complaining often imply that there was a time when he thought he knew how to pray. At some point, everyone who prays confronts this moment when prayer, at first easy and fluid, suddenly becomes arid and laborious. Quite often this is the moment when the Holy Spirit invites the person praying to go from a more exterior, rational or imaginative prayer to a more interior prayer. This is generally also the time when, through the trial of apparent dryness, God invites the one praying to tip over into interiority. Now, this is a crucial passage, which is not always clear and in which the assistance of some accompanist can be very precious. It would be useful to say a few words about this.

Someone who has discovered his interiority has learned to live from his heart. Now, in many cases this passage from the exterior to the interior takes place during prayer. It is part of its history and a decisive step in it. The interior place where God is present in each person, from which he teaches and moves each by what Saint John calls the 'anointing' is progressively revealed to him. Sometimes, this discovery takes place very early, at the very beginning of the life of prayer. In other cases, it occurs at the end of many years; these cases are the more frequent in that our age is still dependent on a formation that put us on guard against feelings and which tended to exalt the so-called 'naked' faith of a kind of voluntaristic rigorism. Already in his day, Saint John of the Cross held that the most fearsome enemies of contemplative prayer were the spiritual directors. In fact, in Spain at the time certain active methods of prayer involving principally reason and imagination were at their peak. From his own experience, John of the Cross had noticed that at a certain moment, all the 'noise' of images and concepts became not only useless at the time of prayer, but even harmful.[15] Only a suspension of this activity, still completely external to the soul, would allow it to listen with its inner ear and to perceive in the deepest part of its heart something radically different. One of the tasks of the accompanist will be to direct

15. John of the Cross, *Living Flame of Love,* Stanza 3, 17-60

the attention of the one praying towards this interior silence where something important is always happening.

As we said above, all accompanists will often be called on by persons who will complain that they no longer know how to pray simply because they are experiencing great difficulties at the time of prayer. They have the impression of wasting their time, and perhaps they have even abandoned—completely or in part—the practice of prayer altogether. We may even think that a good number of Christians, religious included, are more or less in that situation. They have generously explored a number of ways or methods of prayer, each of which succeeded for a while. They have even become more or less familiar with an habitual little daily round with which they are happy for now: a little reading, a bit of reflection or meditation, several invocations, and on the best days, the beginning of a good intention. Why not be content with this, instead of being troublesome to God?

But God is no longer content with this. God has only one means of prying someone out of this daily rut: a small setback from which his love cannot exempt the praying person. To illustrate with an image: he turns the light out and shuts off the tap. God is always present in the person who prays, but from now on elsewhere. It is the only tactic God can use to back someone against a wall and force him to listen there, where God really speaks. From now on he is much closer to the person, but not where the person is used to seeking him. Intelligence, imagination, feelings suddenly all run dry, and the person praying has the unpleasant impression of finding himself up against an insurmountable wall. Everyone knows that such a trial can lead very far and dig very deep. When someone has loyally pledged his whole life to seeking contemplative prayer, a challenge like this can be experienced as a burning failure, as the crumbling of a whole ideal—a little like what we said about the broken mirror. What is more, such a failure risks being immediately followed by an insistent little voice within—the attentive reader now knows whose voice this is: 'No doubt it's your fault; something in your life was not right'. Fortunately, God, who is not accustomed to reserving his graces to those who have fulfilled all the rules, pays no attention to this little voice. And the accompanist will be careful not to pay attention to it either, of course, not even by contradicting it. He need only let it go without arguing against it because what it says is always null and void.

The message the accompanist should try to give on this occasion is this, above all: if prayer seems to have become more difficult, it is not because the person praying has brought this on through his own fault; it is only because God desires this for us. It is the other side of his grace. This is instead an opportunity which we must be ready to catch as it passes by. God is now taking things in hand, he is going more quickly so that the person praying can also follow him more quickly. It is still true such a setback in the life of prayer can be the source of deep dismay. Here the person is, praying at the threshold of a mystery to which he should abandon himself, but not really knowing how to begin or what step to take. Everything is so strange in this world of interiority, completely new to him. Everything seems so upside down from what he was used to feeling and experiencing about God. Once again he needs a guide, not to take him by the hand and push him in a particular direction, but to draw his attention to the mysterious little signs that God is constantly sending him as tangible little signs and proof that he is indeed on the right path and that it is God who is at work in everything that happens to him.

To say that at a particular moment the person praying does not know what step to take next is not correct, because, strictly speaking, there is no step to take, and this is what is both extraordinary and very difficult. Perhaps the most amazing setback God offers him comes when he tries to teach him that he can no longer do anything except abandon himself to God's action. At moments like this, God is very close. There is no longer any step to be taken. There are only a number of things to let fall away, all that obstructs the hands and the heart. He must let go. How to do this, no one can teach or command. One can only suggest it by all one is, because it is quite an art to let oneself tip over completely towards interiority, towards the very depths of one's being which mysteriously opens out onto God. Every believer, in fact, bears in his heart a dizzying abyss which is God. God is present in him as dizziness to which he must abandon himself at some time, by whom he must let himself be seized without holding back by hanging on to some handrail which would promise security against this dizziness.

At these times, the presence of an accompanist is almost always indispensable. His role will be to help the subject become aware of this dizziness without giving in to fear at the absence of familiar landmarks. Otherwise the person praying might run the risk of bypassing the dizziness and circling forever around his own little efforts, becoming more and more bored at prayer time. In this situation, the apprenticeship which is going on cannot be forced: there is no point in precipitating the subject into this dizziness by pushing. It is truly the work of God calling out to the subject's freedom. There is no good time except the one born of the dialogue between grace and freedom. To push someone by force where he does not yet want, or have the means, to go will always be ineffectual. Yet, for all that is reduced, the accompanist's role is no less determinative. His presence may help relax completely fruitless tensions which are a pure waste of time and energy. He can persist in suggesting that one day it will simply come down to a simple abandonment yielding to God's dizziness. Blessed is the person in whose heart the source of prayer has once been able to well up freely, sometimes through a single word, a single gesture, a single glance from a brother whose very discreet intervention has been decisive.

LEARNING HOW TO ACT WITH GOD

We have come to the last crucial point of the whole spiritual experience: learning how to act in constant accord with the action of the Holy Spirit within. In these pages we have already spoken of a more or less frenetic activism which many believers tend to rush into to save themselves far more trying encounters. What is sometimes merely the symptom of human immaturity is more often the sign that these people have not encountered within themselves the movement of the Holy Spirit—by which all their activity could be very peacefully directed. They have yet to learn how to work, not instead of God or even with God, but by letting God work and take the full initiative within them.

'My Father works constantly' *(Jn 5:17)*—this was a secret Jesus confided to his disciples, adding that all his work here below consisted in doing what he saw the Father do. Similarly, God is constantly at work in those he sends, and it would be enough for them to let him act, while trying to encounter his action within them in order to be able to cooperate with him, as he expects. And there would be nothing else to do. Everyone may hope that some day he will be permitted to collaborate this way with grace, thenceforth very differently from the way he used to act at the outset of the spiritual experience. Just as most Christians are frequently tempted to reinvent paths of prayer which suit them and succeed for them, they are in the same way wont to outline to their liking the conditions for acting in the service of the Kingdom. It is God who is constantly at his work, and they are there only as instruments. To be a good instrument, they need only know how to discern within themselves God's activity, which unceasingly tries to take over from our own activity in order to join us completely to his own.

Generally speaking, it is difficult to become aware of the degree to which this presupposes a radical transformation from our usual way of acting. We are so used to working for God with the best of intentions, asking his help in prayer, and sincerely counting on this help throughout our work. But the accent unconsciously rests on the activity of the person who, in his own eyes, seems to be on the job, working on his own projects while counting vaguely on God to guarantee the results, no matter what, because he will have been able to integrate our generous steps into his plan of action. Certainly, God does this and the feverish activism of some people hinders him little in fulfilling his plan of salvation.

But there is a completely different way of working with God, or rather of letting God work in the person who works. In one sense, this way is much easier and indeed more restful for the person involved. And there is no doubt that it gives more glory to God. This privileged way simply consists in becoming capable of tuning into the wavelength—if we may use this comparison—on which God is at work, reaching him on that wavelength and peacefully lending ourselves to his action. No doubt this is what God very much wants to teach human beings, because he is constantly at work in his Church and in the world, both chosen works of his own hands. God is eminently active. To act, he does not wait for man to act first. On the contrary, his power is constantly unleashed on the universe like a hurricane. His activity is present everywhere. It is man who has problems tuning in to it. To continue the same comparison, human activity often develops along a different wavelength. Human programming, our sometimes misplaced activities, may even interfere with the divine programming from time to time. We sometimes have to stop the furious pace of our activities, know how to pause, to put down our weapons and fold our arms, to listen at length to the silence of our hearts. It is at times like these that God's action has some chance of emerging and taking the initiative within us.

This only gives the appearance of being easy, especially

for the active person used to feeding unconsciously on his own activity—as someone gets used to a drug which he cannot stop using without going through withdrawal. This is, in fact, a matter of going from a well-intentioned activism—not without tangible results—to a certain passivity even within action whose effectiveness is not always immediately perceptible. It is a matter, even at the very heart of action, of not getting so caught up in it that the active person not unknowingly cut the thread which binds him to his own interiority, from which all his activity should spring.

Once again, this is not an easy thing to do. To have the ear of one's heart constantly attentive to God's action, continually adjusting oneself to it, remaining in harmony, being joined to it, often presupposes a true crucifixion, a Passover, and most people unconsciously try as long as possible to let the chalice pass by them. Are they not, as it seems to them, absolutely indispensable to the works which in good faith they think they are accomplishing for God? Fortunately, God has no lack of ways to make them put down their weapons and to bring them little by little to unconditional surrender.

This is one last situation where, most of the time, a believer still needs the help of an accompanist to understand the meaning of God's action in his life and the form his intervention takes in his own activities. The impression which the subject will derive from it first is that God is intervening as if to counteract these. Plunged in incomprehension, the believer runs the risk of reacting very awkwardly, with the best intention in the world. The more he should slow down, perhaps even stop for a moment, the more he thrashes about like a maniac. God's action, most often, is strangely disconcerting. Before becoming the rock on which the believer will one day build much more solidly, the divine action is often a scandal and stumbling stone.

The accompanist's role here is extremely important: his

words certainly, but even more his example. He is supposed to be an expert on God's pathways, but correlatively, an expert in his own weakness. In fact, one day he too surprised God, as it were, writing straight on the crooked lines of his poor life. It was difficult, but also important for him, to learn to see how God makes the very best of the miserable rubble he had to offer him. From that moment on, the accompanist was invited to look at his poverty again. He was able to reconcile himself to this insignificance at the sight of the marvels that God constantly worked through him, and this far beyond his limitations and mistakes. And why not, even in spite of his limitations and of all the tricks human beings so often use to try to beat God, to best him on his own field. Is it not to such reconciliation with oneself and God that all accompaniment should lead? And is it not through the infinite patience of one's spiritual father that the person accompanied should learn concretely what it means to collaborate with God's grace: being attentive to it but never presuming on it, following it closely but racing on ahead of it. It is God, and God alone, who never ceases to renew his marvels.

✠

CISTERCIAN TEXTS

Bernard of Clairvaux

- Apologia to Abbot William
- Five Books on Consideration: Advice to a Pope
- Homilies in Praise of the Blessed Virgin Mary
- In Praise of the New Knighthood
- Letters of Bernard of Clairvaux / by B.S. James
- Life and Death of Saint Malachy the Irishman
- Love without Measure: Extracts from the Writings of St Bernard / by Paul Dimier
- On Grace and Free Choice
- On Loving God / Analysis by Emero Stiegman
- Parables and Sentences
- Sermons for the Summer Season
- Sermons on Conversion
- Sermons on the Song of Songs I–IV
- The Steps of Humility and Pride

William of Saint Thierry

- The Enigma of Faith
- Exposition on the Epistle to the Romans
- Exposition on the Song of Songs
- The Golden Epistle
- The Mirror of Faith
- The Nature and Dignity of Love
- On Contemplating God: Prayer & Meditations

Aelred of Rievaulx

- Dialogue on the Soul
- Liturgical Sermons, I
- The Mirror of Charity
- Spiritual Friendship
- Treatises I: On Jesus at the Age of Twelve, Rule for a Recluse, The Pastoral Prayer
- Walter Daniel: The Life of Aelred of Rievaulx

Gertrud the Great of Helfta

- Spiritual Exercises
- The Herald of God's Loving-Kindness (Books 1, 2)
- The Herald of God's Loving-Kindness (Book 3)

John of Ford

- Sermons on the Final Verses of the Songs of Songs I–VII

Gilbert of Hoyland

- Sermons on the Songs of Songs I–III
- Treatises, Sermons and Epistles

Other Early Cistercian Writers

- Adam of Perseigne, Letters of
- Alan of Lille: The Art of Preaching
- Amadeus of Lausanne: Homilies in Praise of Blessed Mary
- Baldwin of Ford: The Commendation of Faith
- Baldwin of Ford: Spiritual Tractates I–II
- Geoffrey of Auxerre: On the Apocalypse
- Guerric of Igny: Liturgical Sermons Vol. I & 2
- Helinand of Froidmont: Verses on Death
- Idung of Prüfening: Cistercians and Cluniacs: The Case for Cîteaux
- In the School of Love. An Anthology of Early Cistercian Texts
- Isaac of Stella: Sermons on the Christian Year, I–[II]
- The Life of Beatrice of Nazareth
- Serlo of Wilton & Serlo of Savigny: Seven Unpublished Works
- Stephen of Lexington: Letters from Ireland
- Stephen of Sawley: Treatises
- Three Treatises on Man: A Cistercian Anthropology

MONASTIC TEXTS

Eastern Monastic Tradition

- Abba Isaiah of Scete: Ascetic Discourses
- Besa: The Life of Shenoute
- Cyril of Scythopolis: Lives of the Monks of Palestine
- Dorotheos of Gaza: Discourses and Sayings
- Evagrius Ponticus: Praktikos and Chapters on Prayer
- Handmaids of the Lord: Lives of Holy Women in Late Antiquity & the Early Middle Ages
- Harlots of the Desert
- John Moschos: The Spiritual Meadow
- Lives of the Desert Fathers
- Lives of Simeon Stylites
- Manjava Skete
- Mena of Nikiou: Isaac of Alexandria & St Macrobius
- The Monastic Rule of Iosif Volotsky (Revised Edition)
- Pachomian Koinonia I–III
- Paphnutius: Histories/Monks of Upper Egypt
- The Sayings of the Desert Fathers
- The Spiritually Beneficial Tales of Paul, Bishop of Monembasia
- Symeon the New Theologian: The Theological and Practical Treatises & The Three Theological Discourses
- Theodoret of Cyrrhus: A History of the

Monks of Syria
- The Syriac Fathers on Prayer and the Spiritual Life

Western Monastic Tradition

- Achard of Saint Victor: Works
- Anselm of Canterbury: Letters I–III / by Walter Fröhlich
- Bede: Commentary…Acts of the Apostles
- Bede: Commentary…Seven Catholic Epistles
- Bede: Homilies on the Gospels I–II
- Bede: Excerpts from the Works of Saint Augustine on the Letters of the Blessed Apostle Paul
- The Celtic Monk
- Gregory the Great: Forty Gospel Homilies
- Life of the Jura Fathers
- The Maxims of Stephen of Muret
- Peter of Celle: Selected Works
- The Letters of Armand Jean-deRancé I–II
- Rule of the Master
- Rule of Saint Augustine

CHRISTIAN SPIRITUALITY

- A Cloud of Witnesses... The Development of Christian Doctrine / by David N. Bell
- The Call of Wild Geese / by Matthew Kelty
- The Cistercian Way / by André Louf
- The Contemplative Path
- Drinking From the Hidden Fountain / by Thomas Spidlík
- Entirely for God / by Elizabeth Isichei
- Eros and Allegory: Medieval Exegesis of the Song of Songs / by Denys Turner
- Fathers Talking / by Aelred Squire
- Friendship and Community / by Brian McGuire
- Grace Can do Moore: Spiritual Accompaniment / by André Louf
- High King of Heaven / by Benedicta Ward
- How Far to Follow / by B. Olivera
- The Hermitage Within / by a Monk
- Life of St Mary Magdalene and of Her Sister St Martha / by David Mycoff
- The Luminous Eye / by Sebastian Brock
- Many Mansions / by David N. Bell
- Mercy in Weakness / by André Louf
- The Name of Jesus / by Irénée Hausherr
- No Moment Too Small / by Norvene Vest
- Penthos: The Doctrine of Compunction in the Christian East / by Irénée Hausherr
- Praying the Word / by Enzo Bianchi
- Praying with Benedict / by Korneel Vermeiren
- Russian Mystics / by Sergius Bolshakoff
- Sermons in a Monastery / by Matthew Kelty

- Silent Herald of Unity: The Life of Maria Gabrielle Sagheddu / by Martha Driscoll
- Spiritual Direction in the Early Christian East / by Irénée Hausherr
- The Spirituality of the Christian East / by Thomas Spidlík
- The Spirituality of the Medieval West / by André Vauchez
- The Spiritual World of Isaac the Syrian / by Hilarion Alfeyev
- Tuning In To Grace / by André Louf

MONASTIC STUDIES

- Community and Abbot in the Rule of St Benedict I–II / by Adalbert de Vogüé
- The Hermit Monks of Grandmont / by Carole A. Hutchison
- In the Unity of the Holy Spirit / by Sighard Kleiner
- A Life Pleasing to God: Saint Basil's Monastic Rules / By Augustine Holmes
- Memoirs [of Jean Leclercq]: From Grace to Grace
- Monastic Practices / by Charles Cummings
- The Occupation of Celtic Sites in Ireland / by Geraldine Carville
- Reading St Benedict / by Adalbert de Vogüé
- Rule of St Benedict: A Doctrinal and Spiritual Commentary / by Adalbert de Vogüé
- The Venerable Bede / by Benedicta Ward
- Western Monasticism / by Peter King
- What Nuns Read / by David N. Bell

CISTERCIAN STUDIES

- Aelred of Rievaulx: A Study / by Aelred Squire
- Athirst for God: Spiritual Desire in Bernard of Clairvaux's Sermons on the Song of Songs / by Michael Casey
- Beatrice of Nazareth in Her Context / by Roger De Ganck
- Bernard of Clairvaux: Man, Monk, Mystic / by Michael Casey [tapes and readings]
- Catalogue of Manuscripts in the Obrecht Collection of the Institute of Cistercian Studies / by Anna Kirkwood
- Christ the Way: The Christology of Guerric of Igny / by John Morson
- The Cistercians in Denmark / by Brian McGuire
- The Cistercians in Scandinavia / by James France
- A Difficult Saint / by Brian McGuire
- The Finances of the Cistercian Order in the Fourteenth Century / by Peter King

- Fountains Abbey and Its Benefactors
  / by Joan Wardrop
- A Gathering of Friends: Learning & Spirituality
  in John of Ford / by Costello and Holdsworth
- The Golden Chain...Isaac of Stella /
  byBernard Mc Ginn
- Image and Likeness: Augustinian Spirituality
  of William of St Thierry / by David Bell
- Index of Authors & Works in Cistercian
  Libraries in Great Britain I / by David Bell
- Index of Cistercian Authors and Works in
  Medieval Library Catalogues in Great Britian
  / by David Bell
- The Mystical Theology of St Bernard
  / by Étienne Gilson
- The New Monastery: Texts & Studies on the
  Earliest Cistercians
- Monastic Odyssey / by Marie Kervingant
- Nicolas Cotheret's Annals of Cîteaux
  / by Louis J. Lekai
- Pater Bernhardus: Martin Luther and
  Bernard of Clairvaux / by Franz Posset
- Pathway of Peace / by Charles Dumont
- Rancé and the Trappist Legacy
  / by A. J. Krailsheimer
- A Second Look at Saint Bernard
  / by Jean Leclercq
- The Spiritual Teachings of St Bernard of
  Clairvaux / by John R. Sommerfeldt
- Studies in Medieval Cistercian History
- Three Founders of Cîteaux
  / by Jean-Baptiste Van Damme
- Towards Unification with God (Beatrice of
  Nazareth in Her Context, 2)
- William, Abbot of St Thierry
- Women and St Bernard of Clairvaux
  / by Jean Leclercq

MEDIEVAL RELIGIOUS WOMEN

A Sub-series edited by
Lillian Thomas Shank and John A. Nichols
- Distant Echoes
- Hidden Springs: Cistercian Monastic Women
  (2 volumes)
- Peace Weavers

CARTHUSIAN TRADITION

- The Call of Silent Love / by A Carthusian
- The Freedom of Obedience / by A Carthusian
- From Advent to Pentecost / by A Carthusian
- Guigo II: The Ladder of Monks & Twelve
  Meditations / by E. Colledge & J. Walsh
- Halfway to Heaven / by R.B. Lockhart
- Interior Prayer / by A Carthusian

- Meditations of Guigo I / by A. Gordon Mursall
- The Prayer of Love and Silence / by A Carthusian
- Poor, Therefore Rich / by A Carthusian
- They Speak by Silences / by A Carthusian
- The Way of Silent Love (A Carthusian Miscellany)
- Where Silence is Praise / by A Carthusian
- The Wound of Love (A Carthusian Miscellany)

CISTERCIAN ART, ARCHITECTURE & MUSIC

- Cistercian Abbeys of Britain
- Cistercian Europe / by Terryl N. Kinder
- Cistercians in Medieval Art / by James France
- Studies in Medieval Art and Architecture
  / edited by Meredith Parsons Lillich
  (Volumes II–V are now available)
- Stones Laid Before the Lord
  / by Anselme Dimier
- Treasures Old and New: Nine Centuries of
  Cistercian Music (compact disc and cassette)

THOMAS MERTON

- The Climate of Monastic Prayer / by T. Merton
- Legacy of Thomas Merton / by P. Hart
- Message of Thomas Merton / by P. Hart
- Monastic Journey of Thomas Merton
  / by Patrick Hart
- Thomas Merton/Monk / by P. Hart
- Thomas Merton on St Bernard
- Toward an Integrated Humanity
  / edited by M. Basil Pennington

CISTERCIAN LITURGICAL DOCUMENTS SERIES

- Cistercian Liturgical Documents Series
  / edited by Chrysogonus Waddell, ocso
- Hymn Collection from the...Paraclete
- The Paraclete Statutes:: Institutiones nostrae
- Molesme Summer-Season Breviary (4 vol.)
- Old French Ordinary & Breviary of the
  Abbey of the Paraclete (2 volumes)
- Twelfth-century Cistercian Hymnal (2 vol.)
- The Twelfth-century Cistercian Psalter
- Two Early Cistercian Libelli Missarum

FESTSCHRIFTS

- Bernardus Magister...Nonacentenary of the Birth of St Bernard
- The Joy of Learning & the Love of God: Essays in Honor of Jean Leclercq
- Praise no Less Than Charity in honor of C. Waddell
- Studiosorum Speculumin honor of Louis J. Lekai
- Truth As Gift... in honor of J. Sommerfeldt

BUSINESS INFORMATION

Editorial Offices & Customer Service

- Cistercian Publications
  WMU Station, 1903 West Michigan Avenue
  Kalamazoo, Michigan 49008-5415   USA

  Telephone 616 387 8920
  Fax   616 387 8390
  e-mail   cistpub@wmich.edu

Please Note: As of 13 July 2002 the 616 area code becomes 269

Canada

- Novalis
  49 Front Street East, Second Floor
  Toronto, Ontario M5E 1B3   CANADA

  Telephone 1 800 204 4140
  Fax   416 363 9409

U.K.

- Cistercian Publications UK
  Mount Saint Bernard Abbey
  Coalville, Leicestershire LE67 5UL   UK

- UK Customer Service & Book Orders
  Cistercian Publications
  97 Loughborough Road
  Thringstone, Coalville
  Leicestershire LE67 8LQ   UK

  Telephone 01530 45 27 24
  Fax   01530 45 02 10
  e-mail   MsbcistP@aol.com

Website

- www.spencerabbey.org/cistpub

Trade Accounts & Credit Applications

- Cistercian Publications / Accounting
  6219 West Kistler Road
  Ludington, Michigan 49431   USA

  Fax   231 843 8919

Cistercian Publications is a non-profit corporation. Its publishing program is restricted to monastic texts in translation and books on the monastic tradition.

A complete catalogue of texts in translation and studies on early, medieval, and modern monasticism is available, free of charge, from any of the addresses above.